Harvard Economic Studies / Volume 133

The studies in this series are published
by the Department of Economics of Harvard
University. The Department does not
assume responsibility for the views
expressed.

Planning Educational Systems for Economic Growth

Samuel Bowles

Harvard University Press
Cambridge, Massachusetts

Preface

This book had its origins in 1960, when my wife and I landed in West Africa to take up positions as education officers in the Government of Northern Nigeria. The two years which I then spent in Nigeria greatly influenced my view of the process of national development, and when I returned to spend another year in 1964, it was to try out a planning model which I had designed to clarify the relationship between educational decisions and economic growth. This research grew into my doctoral dissertation, and the model (but, thankfully, not the dissertation) plays a central part in this book.

In 1966 I was able to spend three months in Greece as an advisor working on problems of educational planning. Although my exposure to Greek education was too limited for me to claim any expertise on the subject, it was helpful in evaluating the generality of some of my impressions formed while working in the educational system of Nigeria.

The intellectual origins of the book lie less in Nigeria and Greece than in Cambridge, Massachusetts, where for the last six years I have intermittently studied and taught economic theory, the economics of education, and other subjects which have a bearing on the optimal use of scarce resources in an educational system.

A book this long in the making should probably contain an appendix in the manner of reports of commissions of inquiry, in which all those who have assisted are fully and gratefully

Preface

acknowledged. But this, I am told, is not done, so I will instead thank only those to whom my debt is particularly heavy.

I am grateful first of all to a series of competent research assistants—James Huntsberger, Jun Onaka, Alice Crampin, and Mathew Lambrinides; they did most of the work. The members and staffs of both the Nigerian Institute of Social and Economic Research in Ibadan and the Center for Planning and Economic Research in Athens contributed greatly in gathering the necessary data. Numerous former colleagues in the Northern Nigerian Ministry of Education, and other friends in Greece as well as in Nigeria taught me most of what I know about education in these two countries.

My original research in Nigeria was financed by the Rockefeller Foundation; since then my work has been funded primarily through a grant by the United States Agency for International Development to the Project for Quantitative Research in Economic Development at Harvard University.

From the beginning I have relied heavily on the advice of my colleagues and friends, particularly on that of Mark Blaug, Hollis Chenery, Robinson Hollister, David Kendrick, Harvey Leibenstein, Henry Levin, Arthur McEwan, Marcelo Selowsky, A. K. Sen, Christopher Sims, and Lester Thurow. I have also benefited greatly from the comments and suggestions of my students. Mary Lombard and Terry Rothra typed the manuscript. I am grateful to them.

This book is dedicated to my wife, Nancy, who is already celebrating its completion; for she knew from the beginning that the attainment of economic efficiency in a school system should not be for long the full-time preoccupation of people interested in education.

Samuel Bowles

Cambridge, Massachusetts
January 1969

Contents

Contents

Contents

Tables

Tables

Figures

Figures

Planning Educational Systems
for Economic Growth

I · Education, Growth, and Planning

This book is about the economics of educational planning. Much of it is devoted to a consideration of the economic characteristics of the production of educated labor in the schools and its use in the economy. This discussion provides the conceptual foundations for a method to determine an efficient allocation of resources in the educational sector. The purposes of education are varied, and the concept of efficiency depends on the particular objectives pursued. Although other goals of education will be considered, I focus primarily on the relationship between education and economic growth. The planning model developed will be estimated and applied in two different economies (Nigeria and Greece) both to illustrate its operation in the context of actual educational policy problems and to permit comparisons to be made with alternative methods of educational planning.

Although the economics of education has an ancient heritage, the idea of using education to accelerate the rate of economic growth is relatively new. The classical economists never doubted the economic importance of education; the concept of investment in human capital is at least as old as *The Wealth of Nations*,[1] and

---

[1] "When any expensive machine is erected, the extraordinary work to be performed by it before it is worn out, it must be expected, will replace the capital laid out upon it, with at least the ordinary profits. A man educated at the expence of much labour and time to any of those employments which require extraordinary dexterity and skill, may be compared to one of those

in that book we find a number of proposed reforms designed to improve the efficiency of resource allocation within the educational system. Yet the classical economists never fully developed the idea that education could be consciously used to stimulate national economic growth; and, in the laissez-faire context of the century following Smith, the need for collective educational planning apparently was not widely felt. If anything, the many schools of economic thought of the late nineteenth and early twentieth centuries devoted less attention to the education-growth relation than did the classical writers.

The recent outburst of interest in this concept, like so many other intellectual developments, is the product of an interaction among new problems, new data, and new tools. Following the Second World War, a number of developments combined to shift the interest of Western economists and public officials from the problem of cyclical fluctuations to economic growth. Heightened competition among the advanced countries, an increased awareness of economic problems in the poor countries, and a growing confidence in counter cyclical policy were all important in creating this shift.

However, the origins of the economics of educational planning appear considerably earlier. It is not surprising that the subject was first systematically treated by an economist in the first major country in modern times to adopt economic growth as a top national priority. In 1925, the Soviet academician S. G. Strumilin estimated the rates of return on various levels of elementary

---

expensive machines. The work which he learns to perform, it must be expected, over and above the usual wages of common labour, will replace to him the whole expence of his education, with at least the ordinary profits of an equally valuable capital. It must do this too in a reasonable time, regard being had to the very uncertain duration of human life, in the same manner as to the more certain duration of the machine." Adam Smith, *The Wealth of Nations,* Cannan edition (New York: Modern Library, 1937), p. 101.

education as part of an overall planning exercise.[2] But if the economics of educational planning was born in the Soviet Union, it apparently did not thrive there. At least a quarter of a century passed with no further major contributions either in Russia or elsewhere.[3]

At the same time, the increased availability of national income estimates and other aggregate economic data along with the growing popularity of empirical estimation of production functions and other economic relations ultimately led to research results which cast serious doubt on the predictive value of the conventional neoclassical theories of economic growth. In the mid-1950's Moses Abramovitz and Robert Solow independently published papers which indicated that increases in capital and labor, as ordinarily measured, accounted for only a relatively small portion of the total observed economic growth of the United States over the first half of the twentieth century.[4] The capacity of the postwar German and Japanese economies to absorb large quantities of physical capital at high levels of productivity when contrasted to the apparently limited absorptive capacity of the poor countries shed further doubt on the adequacy of existing approaches to growth.[5]

[2] S. G. Strumilin, "The Economic Significance of National Education," in E. A. G. Robinson and J. E. Vaizey (eds.), *The Economics of Education* (London: International Economic Association, 1966), pp. 276–323.

[3] For an exception, see J. R. Walsh, "The Capital Concept Applied to Man," *Quarterly Journal of Economics,* February 1935, pp. 255–285.

[4] Moses Abramovitz, "Resource and Output Trends in the U.S. Since 1870," *American Economic Review,* vol. 46, no. 2 (May 1956), pp. 5–34; Robert Solow, "Technological Change and the Aggregate Production Function," *Review of Economics and Statistics,* vol. 39, no. 3 (August 1957), pp. 312–320.

[5] See T. W. Schultz, "Reflections on Investment in Man," *Journal of Political Economy,* October 1962 (supplement), esp. p. 3. Marcelo Selowsky has recently suggested a formal explanation of this phenomenon in terms of the abundance of human capital in Europe and its scarcity in the underdeveloped countries. See his "Educational Capital in a Model of Growth and Distribution" (mimeographed), Economic Development Report No. 88,

It was suspected by many that the portion of growth unexplained by factor accumulation as conventionally measured (or the "residual," as it was called) might in part be attributed to qualitative improvements in the labor force, particularly as affected by increasing levels of educational attainments. The independent work of Edward F. Denison and T. W. Schultz on United States growth in the twentieth century lent some credibility to this view; using different approaches, they estimated that about 20 percent of the growth rate over this period was due to increases in the educational level of the labor force.[6] More recent work by Denison has confirmed these results for many Western European countries.[7] Arnold Harberger and Marcelo Selowsky have come to roughly similar conclusions with respect to Chile.[8]

While the spread of education has undoubtedly been one cause of economic growth in most countries, the reciprocal relationship is also important. The development of general education in the United States and Europe may be due in large part to the rapid rate of economic and social change, which renders it

Project for Quantitative Research in Economic Development, Center for International Affairs, Harvard University, Cambridge, Massachusetts, January 1968.

[6] Edward F. Denison, *Sources of Economic Growth in the U.S. and the Alternatives Before Us* (New York: The Committee on Economic Development, 1962); T. W. Schultz, "Education and Economic Growth," in Nelson B. Henry (ed.), *Social Forces Influencing American Education* (Chicago: National Society for the Study of Education, 1961), pp. 46–88.

[7] Edward F. Denison, *Why Growth Rates Differ: Postwar Experience in Nine Western Countries* (Washington: The Brookings Institution, 1967). However, for a case in which education apparently made a very minor contribution to growth, see Samuel Bowles, "Sources of Growth in the Greek Economy, 1951–1961" (mimeographed), Memorandum No. 27, Development Advisory Service, Center for International Affairs, Harvard University, Cambridge, Massachusetts, April 1967.

[8] Arnold Harberger and Marcelo Selowsky, "Key Factors in the Economic Growth of Chile: An Analysis of the Sources of Past Growth and of the Prospects for 1965–70" (mimeographed), 1966.

4

increasingly difficult to provide adequate socialization and occupational training for youth in the traditional family-, church-, and apprentice-oriented systems of education. In an era characterized by rapid technological change, urbanization, and shifts in the sectoral and occupational distribution of the labor force, the skills of the fathers do not meet the needs of the sons; indeed, the skills sufficient for the sons in their young manhood may be obsolete before they reach middle age. For this reason education and training have become increasingly specialized, their functions carried out by full-time teachers in institutions designed solely for that purpose, that is, in schools. At the same time, the content of education has become increasingly general, with the stress on literacy and the broader aspects of economic and political socialization of youth rather than on specific occupational skills.[9]

It is probably also true that the individual income elasticity of demand for education as a consumer good exceeds one, resulting in the more rapid growth over time of private expenditures on education than of the economy as a whole.[10] Indeed, in a number of countries, education has been viewed less as a contributor to economic growth than as an integral part of the goal of development itself. The spread of mass education, *ipso facto*, is regarded as evidence of growth.

In recent years the educational sector of most countries has been receiving both increasing attention from economists and an

[9] Some writers view adaptation to and diffusion of new technologies as the primary economic function of general education. See, for example, Richard R. Nelson and Edmund S. Phelps, "Investment in Humans, Technological Diffusion, and Economic Growth," American Economic Association, *Proceedings*, May 1966, pp. 69–75.

[10] A cross-section budget study in India, for example, suggests an income elasticity of demand for education of 2.31. A time series for Japan covering the years 1905–1960 yields an estimated 'historical' income elasticity of demand for education of 1.45. See Pierre Ninh Van Tu, "The Economics of Educational Planning," unpub. doc. diss., Australian National University, 1966, pp. 262 and 266.

5

ever larger share of national resources. In the United States, direct expenditures on schooling have been rising at more than twice the rate of growth of the GNP, and, in 1966, they constituted 6 percent of the gross national product. If earnings foregone (indirect expenditures) are included, the figure rises to almost 10 percent. According to estimates by T. W. Schultz, the growth of the human capital stock, as measured solely by educational attainments in the labor force, was twice as rapid as the growth of reproducible tangible capital stock during the period 1929–1957.[11] Annual direct and indirect expenditures on education are approximately of the same magnitude as total, fixed, nonresidential, private gross domestic investment, or about two thirds of private gross domestic investment.[12] At the other end of the income spectrum, India spends almost as much (proportionally) on education. Total direct and indirect expenditures, including earnings foregone, amount to 9 percent of the national income and are almost half the magnitude of gross physical capital formation.[13]

The large amount of resources devoted to education, along with the belief that education is an important cause of economic growth (or at least that the lack of it can be a constraining bottleneck), has resulted in the creation of educational planning units and educational plans in virtually all the major nations of the world. The growth of actual planning operations has been paralleled by the rapid increase in academic interest in educational planning.

[11] T. W. Schultz, *The Economic Value of Education* (New York: Columbia University Press, 1963), p. 51. By comparing a measure of the costs of education which includes foregone student earnings with a measure of national output which does not, I have somewhat overstated the relative magnitude of resource use by education.

[12] Council of Economic Advisors, *Economic Report of the President* (Washington: Superintendent of Documents, 1967), pp. 144, 213, 225. I am using the midpoint of their range of estimates of foregone earnings.

[13] A. M. Nalla Gounden, "Education and Economic Development," unpub. diss., Kurukshetra University (India), 1965, pp. 89–90.

If we restrict our attention to the planning methods actually in widespread use, there are two major types. The first, which may be termed the "social demand approach," amounts to predicting future demand for education by parents and children, ordinarily on the basis of demographic and income trends, and then planning the construction of schools, the training of teachers, and the provision of other inputs to meet these demands. Educational planning in France closely approximates this approach.[14] The second method involves the projection of the occupational and/or educational composition of the labor force to some future date, ordinarily on the basis of estimated sectoral growth rates and productivity changes, and the translation of this projection into required levels of output from the educational system. This method, which I will refer to as the "manpower requirements approach," has been used by the OECD Mediterranean Regional Project in the six southern member countries and is also widely used in the poor countries.[15] An alternative method of educational planning will be suggested in the chapters that follow. This new approach is an attempt to deal systematically with the following major policy issues relating to economic efficiency in the educational sector.

First, is the total amount of resources used by the educational system optimal? Would social welfare be increased by shifting resources from education to production in steel, shirts, or other directly productive activities, or vice versa? Second, what is the socially optimal distribution of resources within the system? Should more resources be devoted to secondary vocational education at the expense of general secondary schools? Should primary education be expanded more rapidly than secondary and higher education? Third, how should education be pro-

[14] Raymond Poignant, "Establishing Educational Targets in France," in *Planning Education for Economic and Social Development* (Paris: OECD, 1963), pp. 205–222.

[15] Herbert S. Parnes, *Forecasting Educational Needs for Economic and Social Development* (Paris: OECD, 1962), p. 113.

duced? Would it be more efficient to reduce the number of years in primary school by lengthening the school year? Should audio-visual methods and other equipment be substituted for teachers? Fourth, if teachers can be imported from abroad and students sent abroad for study, should this be done?

Because educational production is time-consuming, educational plans must extend over a number of years. Therefore, we must ask the above four questions not just once, but for each of the years in the planning period. If we wish to expand secondary school enrollment seven years hence, we must know how many primary school students to admit now, and how many teachers to train, and when, not to mention how many teacher-trainers to educate now, and so on. If we are to devote a given amount of resources to education over an entire planning period, should it be spent equally in each year, or distributed unevenly? Should primary schools be expanded first, and secondary schools later, or the reverse? Should we introduce educational television now, later, or never? In sum, we seek to determine an efficient pattern (over time) of resource use, enrollments, and technological change in the schooling system.

A method of answering the four sets of questions will be developed below and applied to a number of concrete, educational policy issues currently facing the governments of Northern Nigeria and Greece. The distinguishing characteristic of this approach to planning is that it rests on the basic economic principle of maximization subject to constraints. It is thus similar to a number of methods of planning in the economy and will facilitate the ultimate integration of educational and overall economic planning.

The construction of a way to plan the efficient allocation of resources requires a formal quantitative description of two basic economic characteristics of the educational system: its internal productive relationships, and the nature of the demand for its output in the economy at large. Because the choice of an appropriate method of planning will depend directly on our estimates or assumptions concerning these two aspects of the economics of education, the second and third chapters of this book are devoted to a discussion of these issues.

Chapter II deals with some economic aspects of the production of education by the schools and the consumption of schooling by individuals. Chapter III is devoted to an exploration of the use of educated labor in the economy.

An optimizing model for planning is developed in Chapter IV and applied using Northern Nigerian data. The major results of the model concerning the level and distribution of resource use within the educational system, as well as the choice of techniques and the importation of educated labor, are considered.

Chapter V includes a survey of alternative planning methods and a discussion of the differences in policy prescriptions which arise from the use of different models. The application of four alternative planning methods for the Greek educational system will be presented as an illustration.

In Chapter VI the alternative planning methods for education are evaluated in the light both of the empirical comparison in the Greek case study and the experience of other countries.

Although there are a number of shortcomings in the method by which I propose to answer the above questions, my most serious misgivings arise not because I have answered them inadequately, but because they are not the most important questions. Decisions concerning the allocation of resources in education have implications reaching far beyond the conventional concept of economic efficiency. The pattern of development in the educational system will have important effects on the personal distribution of both money income and the nonmonetary benefits of education; thus, issues of equity are necessarily involved. Moreover, the schools influence virtually every aspect of society—from culture and the esthetic environment to the level and form of political participation enjoyed by the citizens. Often the pattern of education most conducive to economic growth is incompatible with important esthetic, ethical, and other values.[16]

The absence in my model of any systematic consideration of issues bearing on the distribution of income and opportunity is certainly the most serious exclusion. This limitation makes the model considerably less interesting than it might otherwise be, particularly to those who share my view that the main economic goal of educational planning ought to be the greater equalization of personal income rather than the increase in total income. Moreover, the political environment in which most educational planning takes place forces planners to take distributional questions seriously, particularly when the educational policies under consideration hold the possibility of reducing the privileges enjoyed by the wealthy and influential.

It should be stressed, therefore, that while the four questions posed constitute the crucial economic efficiency issues involved, there is (and should be) a lot more to educational planning than economic efficiency. The patterns of resource allocation determined by the model are intended to be optimal only with respect to the goal of economic growth. Solutions to the models do not constitute an optimal educational plan; rather, they should be understood as crucial pieces of economic analysis which, together with other types of analysis, are necessary for the intelligent construction of an educational plan.

[16] See, for example, Edgar Z. Friedenberg, *Coming of Age in America—Growth and Acquiescence* (New York: Vintage, 1963).

Note the assumptions by which he concludes that maximizing his welfare function also thereby maximizes growth

II · Outputs and Inputs
in the Educational
Production Process

The economic need for conscious social planning of the educational system arises largely from the peculiar characteristics of the production process of schools and the consumption of their outputs. A discussion of school outputs and the production technology of education will provide an economic rationale for social intervention in educational decision-making and will also establish some guideposts for the later development of planning models for education.

WHAT DO THE SCHOOLS PRODUCE?

The schools in all societies perform a dual function: the selection of young people to fill particular adult roles, and the preparation of such students for adequate performance of these roles. We are concerned here primarily with the preparation, or socialization, function, particularly as it relates to adult occupational roles.[1] The schools develop the cognitive skills and attitudes appropriate for the successful performance of these future tasks.

[1] Talcott Parsons, "The School Class as a Social System: Some of its Functions in American Society," *Harvard Educational Review*, 29 (1959), pp. 297–318. Of course, the socialization function is carried out in a great variety of ways. All societies have educational systems, though many have no schools. For an interesting example of education without schools, see Jomo Kenyata, *Facing Mount Kenya* (New York: Vintage, 1962), pp. 95–124, on the educational system of the Gikuyu; also, Archibald Callaway, "Nigeria's Indigenous Education; the Apprentice System," *Odu*, vol. 1, no. 1 (July 1964), pp. 1–18.

One of the major difficulties in making resource allocation decisions in education is the multidimensional aspect of school output. We may distinguish between the effects of schooling which are primarily economic and those which are primarily noneconomic. Any consequence of the educational system's output which results in an increase in individual welfare can be called a private benefit. It is useful to distinguish between effects which operate via the real income of the individual and those which affect welfare in other ways. I call the former "economic" and the latter "noneconomic," although any dichotomous distinction of this type is bound to be somewhat arbitrary. This classification excludes from the category of economic benefits the consequences of education generally considered to be "consumption benefits," namely, the pleasures of learning or the status and lifestyles that usually accompany education.[2]

Let us consider first the effect of education on personal earnings. This is the major private economic effect of schooling, and the only one which is susceptible to a reasonable degree of accuracy in estimation. The relationship between schooling and personal earnings is illustrated in Figure 1, which presents estimates of the age profile of earnings of workers with different levels of schooling in the United States. Similar data for India and Greece appear in less detail in Figures 2 and 3. All three figures are based on a cross section of individuals at a given point in time. Thus the steepness of the age-earnings profile probably understates the actual increases in earnings which a given

---

[2] The usual "consumption versus investment" distinction in analyzing the output of education appears to rest on a distortion of the usual economic meaning of these terms. Those benefits often referred to as "consumption" accrue to the student throughout his life, and must be viewed as a flow of services resulting from the original acquisition of education. They are thus correctly viewed as returns on an investment. "Consumption benefits" must be those which accrue to the student at the time of purchase of the asset—namely, during the period of schooling itself.

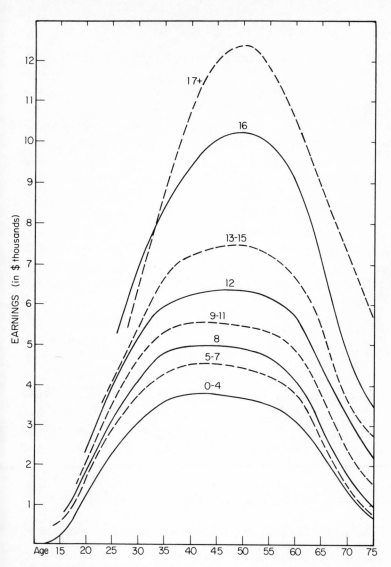

Fig. 1. Estimated Annual Earnings by Age and Schooling: U.S., North, Whites

Source: Giora Hanoch, "Personal Earnings and Investment in Schooling," unpublished doctoral dissertation, University of Chicago, August 1965.

13

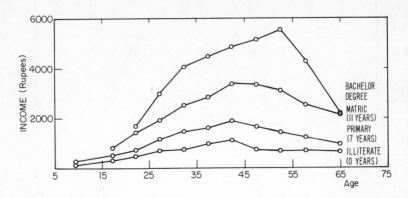

Fig. 2. Estimated Annual Income of Indian Urban Males by Age and Schooling, 1961

Source: A. M. Nalla Gounden, unpublished doctoral dissertation, Kurukshetra University, 1965, p. 69.

individual may expect as he gets older.[3] Subject to this reservation, the effect of education appears to be a higher age profile of earnings, with the initial earnings occurring at a later date, for the better educated.

Although years of schooling and earnings are positively related in all countries for which we have data, it should be remembered that schooling is only one of the many influences on earnings. According to data from the U.S. Census for 1960, differences in years of schooling appear to explain less than a third of the variance of earnings among individuals of the same race, region, sex, and age;[4] in a sample of male Greek workers, education

[3] In the first place, the education received by the older workers in our samples was generally inferior to that now given: thus, our profiles are not really for homogeneous groups. Second, the growth in labor productivity (due to technological progress and capital accumulation) is likely to shift these profiles upward over time.

[4] The U.S. data are reported in Giora Hanoch, "Personal Earnings and Investment in Schooling," unpub. diss., University of Chicago, 1965, pp. 42–47.

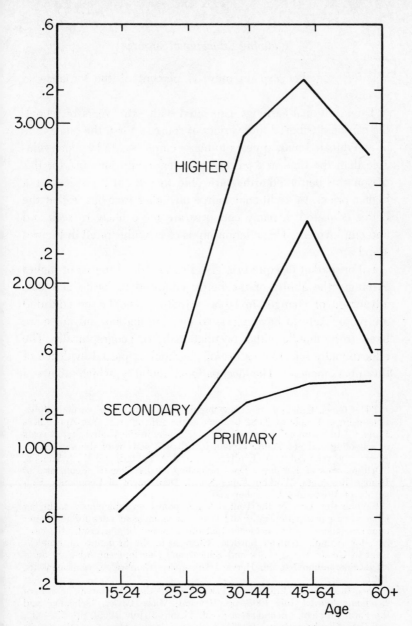

Fig. 3. Annual Earnings by Age and Education as a Fraction of the Earnings of Primary School Graduates Aged 25–29: Greece, 1964

Source: Earnings of males by age group were computed from the raw individual data in a sample of 2,082 workers in the Athens area. These data were collected as a part of a survey directed by Harvey Leibenstein. (See Chap. V.)

and age together explain only 35 percent of the variance in earnings.[5]

The additional earnings associated with extra years of schooling can be attributed to a variety of sources. First, the labor time of an educated man appears to many employers to be more valuable than the time of a worker with less education, and for this reason the better educated are able to sell their services at a higher price. An additional source of higher earnings is that the better educated in many countries are more likely to seek and find employment. This relationship is clearly illustrated in Figures 4 and 5.[6]

Labor market disequilibria give rise to a third source of higher earnings: the ability of the better educated to locate and take advantage of changes in labor scarcities. The better educated are more likely to have access to job information and are more likely to be mobile, either occupationally or geographically. The educationally selective nature of migration is partial evidence of this phenomenon.[7] The occupational mobility which allows a

[5] The Greek finding is from my unpublished estimates of earnings functions using a sample of 2,082 workers in the Athens area. (See Appendices I and V.) In a sample of low scholastic achievers in the United States, years of schooling and age jointly explain less than 7 percent of the variance in earnings, as reported in W. Lee Hansen, B. A. Weisbrod, and W. J. Scanlon, "Determinants of Earnings: Does Schooling Really Count?" Economics of Human Resources, Working Paper No. 5, Department of Economics, University of Wisconsin, December 1967.

[6] While the data for the United States points unambiguously to higher labor force participation rates and lower unemployment rates for the better educated, there is some evidence that this may not be universally the case. See, for example, Samuel Bowles, "Changes in the Structure of Employment in Greece by Age, Sex and Education," Development Advisory Service, Memorandum No. 66, Harvard University, Cambridge, Massachusetts, 1967.

[7] See Rashi Fein, "Educational Patterns in Southern Migration," *Southern Economic Journal,* July 1965, pp. 106–124; Micha Gisser, "Schooling and the Farm Problem," *Econometrica,* vol. 33, no. 3 (July 1965), pp. 582–592; and Otto Klineberg, *Negro Intelligence and Selective Migration* (New York: Columbia University Press, 1935).

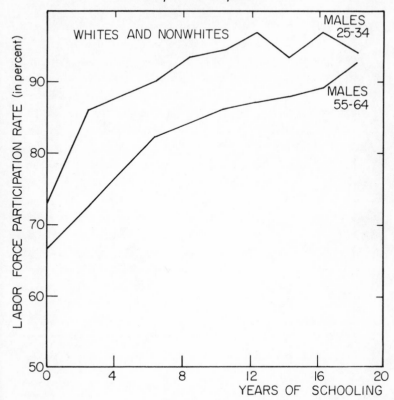

Fig. 4. Schooling and Labor Force Participation in the United States, 1960

Source: U.S. Census of Population 1960 PC(2)5B Table 4.

worker to take advantage of particular scarcities and to avoid being trapped in a glutted occupational market results in part from the greater "trainability" of the better educated.

The greater knowledgeability about jobs and the greater mobility of the educated is merely one example of the complementarity between schooling and other forms of human capital investment, such as vocational training. This constitutes a fourth

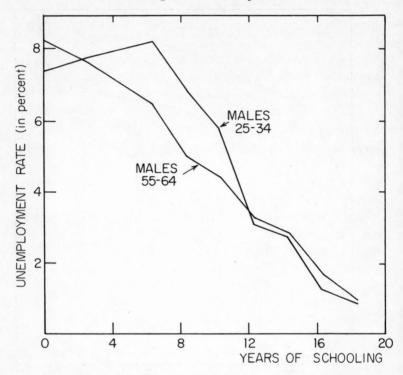

Fig. 5. Schooling and Unemployment, U. S., 1960

Source: U.S. Census of Population 1960 PC(2)5B Table 4.

source of higher earnings. Not only are those with a higher degree of schooling more likely to receive on-the-job training;[8] they are also more likely to invest in their own health, adult

[8] Jacob Mincer, "On the Job Training: Costs, Returns and Some Implications," *Journal of Political Economy*, October 1962 (supplement), tables 1 and 2.

In an unpublished study of occupations in the U.S., Valerie Nelson found that the zero order correlation between median years of schooling in a job and the vocational training requirements of the occupation as estimated by the U.S. Department of Labor was .56.

18

education, and other services which enhance earning capacity.[9] Of course, to the extent that these complementary forms of human capital formation are self-financed, even the sign of the effect on the present value of the net earnings-stream is ambiguous and depends on the rate of return on these investments.

The greater access of better-educated workers to both job information and vocational training and the lower unemployment rates associated with increased schooling suggest that the effect of education on earnings is not only to increase their level but also to reduce their dispersion. Greater earnings security may be regarded as another major benefit of education.

Additional benefits of a nonmonetary but decidedly economic nature ordinarily accrue to an educated individual. Many of the skills learned in school (literacy or dexterity with simple tools, for example) allow the performance of tasks which otherwise would have to be purchased on the market. Burton Weisbrod has estimated that the annual saving to individuals in the United States who are able to make out their own income tax forms is in the neighborhood of $250 million.[10] Additional nonmonetary benefits arise from the fact that a higher level of education ordinarily allows a person to choose an occupation in which on-the-job working conditions are pleasant and vacations relatively long. The low money earnings of college teachers as compared with those of persons of similar educational background in other occupations undoubtedly reflects a voluntary substitution of pleasant working conditions and abundant leisure for higher

[9] See, for example, Selma Mushkin, "Health as an Investment," *Journal of Political Economy*, October 1962 (supplement), p. 131; J. W. Johnstone, *Volunteers for Learning* (Chicago: National Opinion Research Center, 1963); and Lawrence E. Hinkle, Jr., "Occupation, Education, and Coronary Heart Disease," *Science*, vol. 161 (July 19, 1968), pp. 238–246.

[10] Burton A. Weisbrod, *External Benefits of Public Education: An Economic Analysis* (Princeton: Princeton University Press, 1964), pp. 24–26, 28, 30ff.

earnings. (The rationale for calling this effect "economic" is that working conditions and leisure time must be included in a definition of real income.)

The effects of education are not limited to those who receive the schooling; others are often directly affected. We must therefore distinguish between the private benefits which accrue to individual students and the social benefits which accrue to all members of society. Some rewards of the student's education generally come to his parents as well as to his children. In the early years, for example, the school has a custodial function which may serve to liberate the mother for pursuits that are more enjoyable or lucrative than child care. Weisbrod has estimated that the annual value of the custodial service performed by U.S. elementary schools, measured in terms of the expanded employment opportunities for housewives, is $2 billion. Advantages may extend to neighbors or to the general taxpayer in the form of a more desirable community or a reduction in antisocial behavior. These gains may also have some concrete economic manifestations in the reduction in public welfare payments and the costs of police protection. The intergenerational transfer of educational benefits takes a variety of forms. Perhaps the best example is the strong relationship between the educational level of parents and the success of their children in school.[11]

Some of the external benefits may be directly related to production. It has been observed that the better educated are more likely both to invent and to innovate.[12] In view of the fact that successful inventors and innovators seldom capture a monetary

[11] See James S. Coleman, *et al., Equality of Educational Opportunity* (Washington: Superintendent of Documents, 1966), Chap. 3; and Samuel Bowles and H. M. Levin, "More on Multicollinearity and the Effectiveness of Schools," *Journal of Human Resources,* Summer 1968, pp. 3–24.

[12] Jacob Schmookler, "Inventors Past and Present," *Review of Economics and Statistics,* August 1957, pp. 321–333; also, E. M. Rogers, *Diffusion of Innovations* (Glencoe, Illinois: The Free Press, 1962), Chap. 6.

reward equal to the economic effects of their contribution, individual earnings may understate the social contribution of their education.[13]

The above discussion suggests that the personal earnings of workers classified by level of schooling provide only a very rough measure of the benefits of education. But the difficulty is not limited to the problem of externality. Despite the plausibility of the view that the effect of schooling is to increase the economic productivity of individuals, we have very little evidence on this score. The central questions here are: Is well-educated labor more productive than less-educated labor? Are the differences in the productivity of workers, classified by level of schooling, the result of schooling? Or are they attributable to some other cause? [14]

It may be, for example, that in any society there are a certain number of well-paying jobs which are simply seized by the well-educated, not because of a greater capacity to perform them, but because employers reserve well-paying jobs for well-educated people. If this is true, we would have to conclude that the earnings differentials are in fact a good measure of the private economic gain from education but that they cannot serve as a proxy for the social gain, because in this case the schools would serve merely to select those who were to have the high-paying jobs rather than to increase the productivity of the individuals

[13] Of course, in this case individual earnings must overstate the social productivity of some other workers. A. K. Sen has pointed out to me that if those who capture the returns of innovation are, on the whole, better educated than the innovators themselves, relative earnings will overstate the social returns on some levels of education.

[14] These two questions have aroused some controversy among economists. For a good survey of the points of contention see Mark Blaug, "The Rate of Return on Investment in Human Capital in Great Britain," *The Manchester School,* September 1965, pp. 205–251. For a view critical of the approach taken here, see Thomas Balogh and Paul Streeten, "The Coefficient of Ignorance," *Bulletin of the Oxford University Institute of Economics and Statistics,* May 1963, pp. 99–107.

performing the jobs. Furthermore, even if it turned out that educated labor was in fact more productive than uneducated labor, it would be necessary to take account of the probability that because of their intelligence, motivation, and other characteristics, the types of people who normally receive a higher level of schooling would be more productive than the uneducated even in the absence of schooling.

We take up these two problems in turn. Recent econometric work on production functions suggests that the quality of labor, measured by years of schooling completed, exerts a large and statistically significant influence on production.[15] The evidence that well-educated labor is more productive than less-educated labor is direct and compelling.

Moreover, the behavior of firms which are willing to pay substantially more for a relatively well-educated worker suggests that they, at least, perceive some productive difference. Of course, it may be that educated labor is not in fact more productive, and that the employment of educated labor at higher wages is some sort of irrational "conspicuous production." But if we are to accept the extreme view that education is not produc-

[15] See, particularly, Zvi Griliches, "Estimates of the Aggregate Agricultural Production Function from Cross Section Data," *Journal of Farm Economics,* vol. 45, no. 2 (May 1963), appendix, table 6; "Agricultural Production Functions," *American Economic Review,* December 1964, pp. 961–974; "Production Functions in Manufacturing: Some Preliminary Results," in Murray Brown (ed.), *The Theory and Empirical Analysis of Production,* Studies in Income and Wealth, vol. 31 (New York: National Bureau of Economic Research, 1967), pp. 275–322; Murray Brown and Alfred H. Conrad, "The Influence of Research and Education on CES Production Relations," in Murray Brown (ed.), *The Theory and Empirical Analysis of Production,* pp. 241–272; and D. P. Chaudhri, "Education and Agricultural Productivity in India," unpub. Ph.D. diss., University of Delhi, April 1968. Other studies, using an index of years of schooling completed weighted by the relative annual earnings of the schooling classes in question give similar results. For a review of the evidence, see Zvi Griliches, "Notes on the Role of Education in Production Functions and Growth Accounting," paper delivered at the Conference on Education and Income of the National Bureau of Economic Research, November 1968.

tive, we must be prepared to believe, for example, that, in 1959, U.S. employers were willing to pay $43 billion, or over a fifth of the total male labor earnings, for the privilege of hiring labor with more than eight years of schooling for jobs that elementary school graduates could have done just as well.[16]

In fact, if the firms maximize profits, and if labor markets are perfect, the hiring of various types of labor should continue until the respective marginal productivities are proportional to the wages for each type of labor. (Having any other amount would result in lower profits. When both product and labor markets are perfect, wages will equal the value of the marginal product.) The fact that some wages may be fixed by law (as in some low-paying jobs) or by convention (as in some professions) does not alter the basic argument.[17] Firms can simply adjust their employment of the factor to the given wage. The appearance of excess demand or a significant amount of unemployment for a particular type of labor at the given wage will set under way pressures for the alteration of factor prices.

Those who find the above argument implausible often contend that the economic behavior of firms and other economic units is governed more by convention than by any rational optimization such as that underlying most of contemporary microeconomic theory. This is undoubtedly true and perhaps particularly true in the agricultural sectors which dominate the economies of most poor countries. But to conclude that the pervasiveness of conventional behavior rather than conscious optimization, invalidates market evidence of relative factor productivities is to misunderstand the basic theory and to overlook a considerable

---

[16] U.S. Census, 1960, Earnings by Education and Occupation, PC(2)–7B. Our hypothetical calculation refers only to male workers and is based on the definition of labor earnings used in the cited census volume.

[17] A wage fixed in the short run, in fact, strengthens the argument to the extent that it eliminates the possibility of a divergence between the marginal and average cost of acquiring an additional unit of labor.

amount of information on the economic content of "conventional" behavior. For the crux of the microeconomic theory germane to this question maintains only that economic agents allocate resources as if by a conscious rational process, whatever the actual thought processes involved. And there is a considerable and growing body of data to the effect that the resource allocation in peasant agriculture, though governed in large measure by convention, is often highly rational, given the available inputs.[18]

Even in societies with administered factor prices we find evidence that market prices carry some information concerning the relative scarcity of factors of production. Thus, for example, in Israel, where the wage structure is dominated to a considerable degree by the Histadrut, the short-run movements in the relative prices of skilled and unskilled labor appear to conform closely to our *a priori* expectations, given the sharp changes in the skill composition of the labor force during the 1950's.[19] Likewise, in the sample of countries discussed in the next chapter, many of which are thought to have "rigid" or conventional wage structures, we observe a relationship between relative factor payments and relative factor quantities, which, while small in magnitude, is consistently negative, as would be expected from our highly simplified microeconomic theory of the labor market.

---

[18] For example: T. W. Schultz, *Transforming Traditional Agriculture* (New Haven: Yale University Press, 1964), pp. 36–52; Benton Massell, "Econometric Variations on a Theme from Schneider," *Economic Development and Cultural Change,* vol. 12, no. 1 (October 1963), pp. 34–41; W. D. Hopper, "The Allocative Efficiency in Traditional Indian Agriculture," *Journal of Farm Economics,* August 1965, pp. 611–624; W. P. Falcon, "Farmer Response to Price in a Subsistence Economy: The Case of West Pakistan," *American Economic Review* (Proceedings), 54 (May 1964), pp. 580–591; and Carl H. Gotsch, "Technological Change and Private Investment in Agriculture: A Case Study of the Pakistan Punjab,' unpub. diss., Harvard University, 1967.

[19] U. Bahral, *The Effect of Mass Immigration on Wages in Israel* (Jerusalem: Israel Universities Press, 1965).

The above evidence is ample to support the proposition that educated labor is indeed more productive than uneducated labor. But we have extended the argument somewhat by suggesting that the relative earnings of labor educated at different levels correspond roughly to the relative scarcities, or relative marginal products, of the various categories of workers. I do not propose that there is a one to one correspondence between factor prices and marginal products. I know of no evidence which could conceivably substantiate this view. Nonetheless, there are undoubtedly numerous cases of significant divergence between relative wages and relative marginal products. The pay differential between black and white labor of the same age and level of schooling in the United States would seem to provide a good example. Examples of a major divergence, however, are probably more likely to appear over short periods of time in fairly narrowly defined occupational groups than they are over decades in the major educational categories. In any case, the evidence seems sufficiently strong to use the earnings of broad educational categories of workers as rough approximations of marginal products, particularly in a model which facilitates analysis of the sensitivity of the results to deviations from this assumption.

Even if relative earnings are a good measure of the relative marginal productivities of labor grouped by educational level, we cannot yet be sure that the differences in productivity reflect the unique contribution of schooling. The available evidence on this problem, all pertaining to the United States, suggests that there are significant increments in earnings associated with additional education which cannot be accounted for by a positive association between the level of schooling, on the one hand, and intelligence, parents' occupation and scholastic achievement, on the other. A number of studies indicate that at least 60 percent, and, in some cases, a much higher percentage, of the earnings differences among workers classified by education are not due to these "non-schooling" effects.[20]

Most economists and educators will accept the proposition that education makes some contribution to productivity; few, understandably, seek to explain why this is so. Our knowledge of the relationship between education and productivity is still primitive. I suspect that the answer lies not in the occupational skills transmitted by the schools, but in the ability of the educational system to equip youth successfully to fill adult roles, occupational or otherwise. This socialization function of education accounts for the greater ability of the educated to cope with their entire environment. Successful performance of a job requires many of the same attitudes that are required for success in all roles: discipline, ability to communicate, and some basic reasoning capabilities, for example.[21] The school is particularly important as a socializing institution in many poor countries, where training within the family and other traditional socialization agencies is

[20] The data on this question are highly unsatisfactory. Gary Becker provides a useful summary in *Human Capital* (New York: National Bureau of Economic Research, 1964), pp. 79–88. See also Edward F. Denison, "Proportion of Income Differentials Among Education Groups Due to Additional Education," *The Residual Factor and Economic Growth* (Paris: OECD, 1965), pp. 86–100; Burton Weisbrod and Peter Karpoff, "Monetary Returns to College Education: Some New Evidence," unpub., 1967; and James Morgan and Martin David, "Education and Income," *Quarterly Journal of Economics,* August 1963, pp. 423–437. It should be pointed out that in all studies the "unique" effect of education on earnings is arrived at as a residual—that is, after correcting for nonschooling influences on earnings. Thus, the estimates must be strictly interpreted to represent the unique contribution of schooling, plus the influence of any nonmeasured variables which are correlated with both earnings and level of schooling. The only results which suggest a rather small unique contribution of schooling were arrived at by a process which considerably overcorrects for the influence of nonschooling factors—for example, by holding the amount of administrative responsibility constant.

[21] An elaboration of the view that the contribution of schooling to production does not operate primarily via cognitive development can be found in Herbert Gintis, "Towards a Method in the Economics of Education: The Educational Production Function," unpub., January 1969.

inadequate for successful performance in the modernizing sectors of these nations. It may not be an exaggeration to suggest that from the employer's standpoint, the main function of primary education is not to enlighten, or to impart particular job skills, but to teach youth to come on time, to adjust to boring routine, and to take orders from someone outside the family or traditional system of authority. Methods of teaching and the administration of authority within the schools often seem ideally—and sometimes even exclusively—suited to these goals.[22] A similar view of the economic function of education is probably roughly applicable to postprimary education, and, for that matter, to schooling everywhere.

This does not mean, of course, that schooling is unrelated to the process of skill acquisition. Employers are willing to pay higher salaries to well-educated workers not so much for the skills they have learned in school, but for their facility for learning on the job, their ability to adjust to rapidly changing job content, and because of the lower costs of training them for the performance of particular occupational roles. If this interpretation is correct, the economic function of the school is to develop the values and commitments as well as the basic abilities which enhance a worker's trainability and on-the-job learning capacity.[23]

The consequences of education will not always be to increase social or individual welfare. Negative effects, or costs associated with outputs rather than inputs, may be of considerable impor-

[22] On the importance of school structure in the socialization process, see Robert Dreeben, *On What is Learned in School* (Reading, Mass.: Addison Wesley, 1968).

[23] Needless to say, the above reasoning is more applicable to some types of education and to some occupations than to others. If true, it suggests at least one explanation of the following paradox. Those types of schooling most consciously oriented toward economic objectives, ordinarily at the expense of other educational goals—namely, vocational education—are often the least profitable when evaluated in terms of purely economic criteria. For example, see Chapters IV and V.

tance. Education may give rise to attitudes toward manual labor or work in rural areas that introduce rigidities into the labor market and contribute to the problem of the unemployment of educated labor—thus reducing the allocative efficiency of the economy.[24] Negative effects of a noneconomic type are undoubtedly important to some groups, particularly in countries undergoing a process of rapid modernization.

HOW IS EDUCATION PRODUCED?

Knowledge of the relation between inputs and outputs in the schools is an essential part of any planning approach to education. Without knowledge of the educational production process, we are unable to estimate the relative effectiveness of each factor input per unit of cost; nor are we able to compare the relative productivity of resources devoted to different types of educational or noneducational purposes. Unfortunately, even in the United States, with its wealth of educational data, the underlying relationships between school inputs and school outputs are largely unknown.[25] In the absence of empirical estimates of the production functions for education, we must rely on the judgment of those involved in the production process itself—the educators.

Four characteristics of the educational production process are

[24] These and other negative effects have received little attention in the literature on education and economic growth. See, however, Gordon C. Ruscoe, *Dysfunctionality in Jamaican Education* (Ann Arbor: University of Michigan, School of Education, 1963); and John Vaizey, "Some of the Main Issues in the Strategy of Educational Supply," *Policy Conference on Economic Growth and Investment in Education,* Washington, October 16–20, 1961 (Paris: OECD, 1962), p. 52.

[25] See, for example, Samuel Bowles, "Towards an Educational Production Function," paper presented at the conference of the National Bureau of Economic Research on Education and Income, November, 1968; and Samuel Bowles and H. M. Levin, "The Determinants of Scholastic Achievement— An Appraisal of Some Recent Evidence," *Journal of Human Resources,* Winter 1968, pp. 3–24.

particularly relevant for the choice of an educational planning technique. The first is the very small amount of actual substitution between inputs in the production process. The degree of substitutability between inputs which is possible from a purely technological (pedagogical) point of view is probably considerable. Educational television allows the substitution of equipment for teachers with particular skills, while team teaching and similar organizational innovation allow some substitution among teachers in various grades. Of greater relevance in the poor countries is a wide range of substitutability between the quality and quantity of teachers and the availability and quality of textbooks. Students' time and teachers' time are to some extent substitutable; the same amount may be taught by spreading fewer teacher hours over more student hours.

Despite the wide range of substitutions that are apparently possible, the limited variability in the observed per student inputs suggests that a common production technology is generally used, at least within the boundaries of the political subdivisions responsible for administering education. The similarity in production techniques in use probably reflects the view among educational administrators that at any given time the appropriate input coefficients are roughly fixed and that all schools of a given type should conform to the same general standards.[26] In this respect an educational project is not too different in the planner's eyes from, say, a modern petrochemicals complex whose well-defined set of manpower requirements is established (by engineers) prior to the planner's economic analysis.

A second salient feature of educational production processes is their long period of production. All production processes are time-consuming; but where the production period is relatively

[26] These standards are ordinarily expressed in legal instruments or administrative regulations. The process of conforming to these rules generally produces a quite uniform input structure.

short, as in agriculture and most of manufacturing, we generally ignore the time dimension. A single educational production process may extend over as many as eight years. Extremely time-consuming economic activities, like the construction of dams, bridges, and irrigation systems, require special treatment. Similarly, planning techniques in education must take time explicitly into account.

The third important characteristic of educational production is the degree of interdependence among different types of educational institutions. The educational system is its own major supplier of inputs (in the form of teachers and students continuing their education). From the planning standpoint, it is most fruitful to regard the educational sector of the economy as an aggregation of each individual school's production process, comprising a unified production system. Planning resource allocation in education requires an understanding of the complicated net of interdependencies within the system. We must know the relationship between planned enrollments now and the resulting deliveries to the labor force later; between planned admissions to one level in the future and admissions to teacher-training and feeder schools now. It will be seen in Chapter IV that an intertemporal input-output model provides a useful framework in which to understand the structural interdependence within the educational sector. Because most educational activities simultaneously produce students to be admitted at the next higher level and teachers for the lower levels, as well as new recruits for the labor force, the classification of educational processes in the usual economic trichotomy—capacity creators, intermediate goods suppliers, and final demand suppliers—cannot be specified in advance, but depends on the optimal solution to the educational planning problem.[27]

[27] It will be seen in Chapters IV and V that the optimal solution ordinarily does imply an unambiguous classification, one, in fact, which is reminiscent of the ordering of capital goods in Austrian capital theory.

The fourth characteristic of the production of education which is important from the standpoint of planning is the degree to which the factors of production are specific to the educational sector. School buildings and equipment are obviously specific. Although to a lesser degree, most types of teachers are specific, in the sense that the performance of their jobs requires training or skills which are of limited usefulness outside education.

THE COSTS OF SCHOOLING

The production technology of the entire educational system provides the framework for the estimation of the costs of schooling. For the purposes of determining efficient patterns of resource allocation, the cost of education should be a money measure of the opportunities which society must forego in order to obtain an additional unit of schooling. The concept appropriate for planning purposes is social rather than private cost. The cost of education to the school or the student is not the relevant figure, since it includes items of private as well as of social cost—such as feeding the students and perhaps housing and clothing them —services which, if not undertaken at school, would have to be undertaken at home. Naturally, if the marginal cost of these services when provided by the school differs from their marginal cost when provided at home, the difference (positive or negative) should be attributed to education. Conversely, the costs borne by the school exclude some which represent real social opportunities foregone: for example, the rent-free use of urban land or the withdrawal of students from the labor force for the continuation of their education. Students' time should be valued at its opportunity cost, namely, the social marginal productivity of a student if he were on the labor market.[28] Measurement of

[28] In measuring the opportunity cost of student time solely in terms of foregone social marginal productivity in employment (such as earnings), we are assuming that the productivity lost to the economy is not offset, even

the social marginal productivity of the student were he to seek employment must include consideration of his employment prospects and the effects of his entry into the labor force on employment and productivity elsewhere.[29] The inclusion of the opportunity cost of students' time in the cost-of-education concept is by no means a minor adjustment. Recent studies of education costs in Israel, India, Mexico, and the United States indicate that the foregone earnings of the students constitute between half and two thirds of the total costs of secondary and higher education.[30]

---

in part, by the psychic pleasure of studying as opposed to working. We assume that the student is indifferent as between these two forms of activity.

[29] It is sometimes suggested that the relevant measure is the social marginal productivity of the student if all students were to enter the labor market. Weisbrod points out that this implies the consideration of drastic policy alternatives: "Studies involving the costs and benefits of education are surely not directed to the question of whether there should or should not be education. The issue is whether fewer or more people should be encouraged to go further in school. Only marginal changes are being contemplated." "Education and Investment in Human Capital," *Journal of Political Economy*, vol. 70, no. 5, part 2 (October 1962), appendix, p. 122. He suggests that the problem of the unemployment of nonstudents should not be considered at all in estimating the opportunity costs of students' time, as the problem of allocative efficiency in education should not be confused with the problem of achieving full employment. This approach appears to be unfounded. It is no more legitimate to assume full employment than to assume any other level in calculating the opportunity costs. From the planning standpoint, it makes sense to assume a range of likely rates of unemployment, rather than the most desirable rate.

[30] A. M. Nalla Gounden, "Education and Economic Development; A Study in Human Capital Formation and Its Role in Economic Development in India, 1950–51—1960–61," unpub. diss., Kurukshetra University (India), November 1965, p. 83; Martin Carnoy, "The Cost and Return to Schooling in Mexico: A Case Study," unpub. diss., University of Chicago, September 1963, p. 23; T. W. Schultz, "Education and Economic Growth," in N. B. Henry (ed.), *Social Forces Influencing American Education* (Chicago: University of Chicago Press, 1961), pp. 62–63; T. W. Schultz, *The Economic Value of Education* (New York: Columbia University Press, 1963), p. 29; and Carl Shoup, *et al., The Fiscal System of Venezuela,* A Report of the Commission to Study the Fiscal System of Venezuela (Baltimore: The Johns Hopkins Press, 1959), pp. 406–409.

WHY PLAN EDUCATION?

Few societies have ever left educational decision-making entirely in the hands of the individuals most intimately involved. This may in part reflect the fact that education plays a crucial role in the selection and training of social elites, and it has generally been in the interest of these groups to exercise some control over its distribution and content. Though the major motivation for social intervention in the educational process may thus be, broadly speaking, political, there are good economic reasons why completely individual choice in the production and consumption of education is socially undesirable.

There is in general a major divergence between the private and social benefits and costs of education. Given the present almost universal commitment of public support to education, the full social costs are not usually borne by the student, but are distributed among him, his family, the school, and other social agencies; the benefits of an individual's education are also distributed among a large number of people. Decisions relating to schooling are made more difficult because of imperfect information, both about the student's own talents and about the future returns to education. This problem is exacerbated by the fact that most schooling decisions are made by, or at least for, people who are still young, at a time when their abilities and preferences are still subject to drastic change, and when they have a long uncharted life stretching half a century or so ahead of them. Evaluation of benefits over this length of time is exceedingly difficult. Moreover, the trial-and-error process by which information is ordinarily acquired in many consumption activities is virtually impossible. Because the effects of education are embodied in a human being, any particular form of human capital investment is made only once. And as a further consequence of the embodiment phenomenon, the resulting human capital asset can never be sold; thus schooling decisions are irrevocable.

This suggests that a market solution to resource allocation in education would not be efficient, even in the static *Pareto optimum* sense. (Of course, it might be more efficient than many of the centralized bureaucratic allocation processes found in educational systems around the world.) In any case, even if we were roughly satisfied with the equilibrium allocation resulting from such an arrangement, we would have to inquire about the adjustment mechanism whereby the equilibrium is to be achieved. The long duration of most educational courses and the extreme interdependency of the parts of the educational system suggest that even in the best of possible circumstances adjustment to disequilibria would be a slow process. Indeed, in most countries on which data are available there are indications that the human capital market is significantly out of equilibrium, both from a private and a social standpoint. For some types of education, wide oscillation around the equilibria values on the cobweb cycle pattern is a distinct possibility.[31]

The last important shortcoming of a purely market solution to resource allocation in education is that the educational system is expected to alter tastes and values. Thus, individual schooling decisions, based on a pre-education set of preferences, may appear undesirable in terms of post-education preferences.

Our discussion of the economic characteristics of education

[31] K. J. Arrow and W. M. Capron, "Dynamic Shortages and Price Rises: the Engineer-Scientist Case," *Quarterly Journal of Economics,* vol. 73, no. 2 (May 1959), pp. 292–308; D. M. Blank and G. J. Stigler, *The Demand and Supply of Scientific Personnel* (New York: The National Bureau of Economic Research, 1957); Richard Freeman, "An Economic Analysis of Scientific and Engineering Manpower," unpub. doc. diss., Harvard University, Cambridge, Massachusetts, March 1968.

provides compelling reasons for rejecting the unplanned market approach to educational resource allocation. It also provides some suggestions as to an appropriate method of planning. First, because of the multidimensional and only partially measurable nature of the output of schooling, an approach to educational planning which can be used to measure the economic implications of following a number of different strategies and which allows for the estimation of the trade-offs among competing objectives is more useful than a deterministic model which yields only a single solution. We would like a planning model which could generate educational plans based on, say, nationalistic, as well as economic growth, objectives. Such a model would allow us to evaluate some of the political costs associated with the unmitigated pursuit of economic growth as well as the degree to which growth might be jeopardized by the pursuit of extreme nationalistic policies in education.

Second, because of the time-consuming nature of the educational production process and the embodiment of the effects of schooling in relatively long-lived human beings, an intertemporal approach is needed.

Third, because of the limited range of actual substitution in the production of education, the long production period, the fact that the most important inputs into schools are the products of the educational system itself, and the specific nature of many inputs, both the supply and the demand for educational inputs are relatively inelastic. For this reason what can accurately be called bottlenecks often develop in the process of educational expansion. When they occur, the social marginal productivity of the educational inputs in question often greatly exceed their market cost. In this situation the costs of inputs when valued at market prices (even taking into account the private cost-social cost distinction) are likely to be a very poor reflection of the real social-opportunity costs of these inputs. (This will be seen in

Chapter IV, where the shadow price of some inputs greatly exceeds the market cost.)

For an approach to educational planning to take account of these divergences, it must include the educational production processes explicitly in the framework of a general model of the system. Moreover, inputs into the schooling processes must be measured in physical rather than in value units whenever possible.

To conclude, the material presented in this chapter suggests the following two propositions, which, despite extreme simplicity and undertones of schizophrenia, to my mind constitute an adequate representation of those aspects of the relationship between education and the economy relevant to the construction of a planning model for education. First, the labor market is in equilibrium, in the sense that factors are paid roughly the value of their marginal product. This assumption allows us to measure the economic benefits of schooling. Second, the human capital market, particularly as it relates to schooling, is, for a variety of reasons, generally out of equilibrium: there are potential changes in the educational composition of the labor force which, taking into account the associated costs, would allow an increase in the present value of future national income. The disequilibrium of the human capital market provides the rationale for an economic approach to educational planning.

III · The Long-run Demand
for Educated Labor

In order to develop a comprehensive planning method for the education sector, we must be able to represent quantitatively the economywide demand for the outputs of the schools. This information will provide the basis for choosing the optimal set of educational outputs from among the multitude of feasible sets. The method chosen to measure the economy's demand for educated labor will greatly influence the ultimate form of the educational planning model.

If (to take one of the two polar cases) the economy demands labor with various levels of schooling in rigidly fixed proportions, then the desired outputs of the educational system at any future date can be determined solely on the basis of the desired level of production of goods and services in the economy and of the expected retirements from the existing stock of labor. The function of the educational system in this case is to match the educational attainments of the labor force with the fixed input requirements generated by the economy. If, however, it is possible to substitute one type of labor for another in production, then the above method breaks down, for it is no longer possible to derive the "demands" for each type of labor solely from the level of total output.

Turning to the alternate polar case, let us assume that there is such a high degree of substitutability among factors in the economy that the relative marginal products of each type of labor remain constant, regardless of the available amounts of each factor. In this case, we could compute the contribution to the present value of the future stream of national income for each type of schooling and choose from the feasible sets of enrollment levels the educational plan that yielded the largest total contribution to national income. If, however, the marginal product functions for each type of labor are downward sloping, we cannot determine the contribution of each type of education to national income until we know which set of enrollments is to be chosen.

In the first case the educational plan is determined directly by the technologies in the economy and an exogenously specified rate of growth, while in the second it is based on choice among competing uses of scarce resources. For this reason I will refer to the planning method implied by the first case as "technological" and to that implied by the second as "economic." The solution to resource allocation problems in either polar case presents few computational difficulties. It is clear that intermediate cases are far less simple. Virtually all operational methods of educational planning have relied, at least implicitly, on the "technological" case. Yet the available evidence is inconsistent with the basic underlying assumption, namely, that labor inputs must be used in fixed proportions. The data which I will present demonstrate that different types of labor are in fact highly substitutable. In Chapter IV a planning model based on the "economic" case will be constructed, estimated, and operated.

The Elasticity of Demand for Educated Labor

The relationship between the amount of a given type of labor available in an economy and its marginal contribution to national income (or social marginal productivity) is defined as the aggregate demand function for that type of labor. The concept is analogous to the firm's demand function for a factor in that it represents for each amount of the factor the maximum which a national income-maximizing planning agency should be willing to pay in order to acquire one additional unit.[1] The shape and position of this aggregate demand function depend on the characteristics of the sectoral production functions, the level and elasticity of demand for the sectoral outputs, and the availability of complementary and substitute factors. In order to distinguish between the two extreme cases presented in the previous section, we introduce the concept of the elasticity of demand for educated labor, E_i, or the inverse of the percentage change in the marginal product of factor i associated with a given percentage change in the amount available.

$$E_i \equiv \frac{dN_i/N_i}{dMP_i/MP_i}$$

The relationship assumed in the above cases between the marginal contribution to national income of a given category of labor and the amount of labor available appears in Figures 6 and 7. The greater the elasticity of demand is, the less the marginal productivity of the factor will vary with the amount of it available; the situation will more nearly approach that described as polar

[1] The demand for educated labor should be clearly distinguished from what might be called the individual demand for education, which relates the amount of education desired by an individual to the price of education and which depends on variables such as anticipated future returns (monetary and otherwise) to the individual and his rate of time preference. The demand for education in this latter sense will not be discussed here. In view of the fact that schooling is generally either free or offered at highly subsidized rates, it can be assumed that the private return to education will be sufficiently high to allow government bodies to regulate the amount of schooling undertaken at each level through regulation of available places, supplemented occasionally by relatively minor financial inducements. Deficient demand for education is not regarded as a problem.

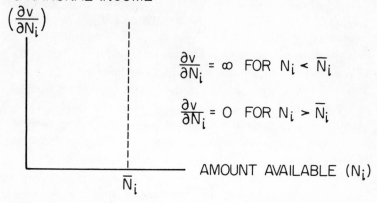

MARGINAL CONTRIBUTION
TO NATIONAL INCOME

$$\left(\frac{\partial v}{\partial N_i}\right)$$

$$\frac{\partial v}{\partial N_i} = \infty \quad \text{FOR} \quad N_i < \overline{N}_i$$

$$\frac{\partial v}{\partial N_i} = 0 \quad \text{FOR} \quad N_i > \overline{N}_i$$

AMOUNT AVAILABLE (N_i)

$\overline{N}_i$

Fig. 6. The "Technological" Case: Labor Inputs Required in
Fixed Proportions

case two, where the elasticity of demand is infinite. The contrary
situation (case one) implies an elasticity of demand equal to
zero.

The elasticity of demand for a factor will be greater: the
greater the elasticity of substitution between it and other factors
in production; the greater the elasticity of demand for the product or products which it produces; and the greater the elasticity
of the supply of factors of production which may serve as substitutes for the factor in question.[2]

[2] Alfred Marshall, *Principles of Economics* (London: Macmillan, 1961),
Book V, Chap. 6, pp. 385–386. For a two-factor model, the relationship
between the elasticity of demand for a factor, on the one hand, and the
price elasticity of demand for the output and the elasticity of substitution between factors, on the other, is found in R. G. D. Allen, *Mathematical Analysis for Economists* (London: MacMillan, 1962), p. 372. With many factors,
the concept of the elasticity of substitution is inappropriate and must be replaced by some concept of the "partial" elasticity of substitution. Although
the formal expression for the elasticity of demand for the factor is thus
altered, the economic considerations leading to a high or a low elasticity

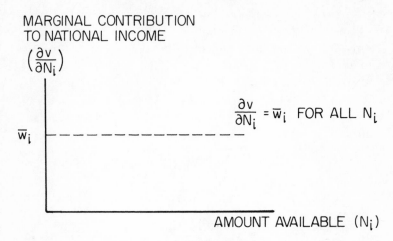

MARGINAL CONTRIBUTION
TO NATIONAL INCOME
$\left(\dfrac{\partial v}{\partial N_i}\right)$

$\dfrac{\partial v}{\partial N_i} = \bar{w}_i$ FOR ALL N_i

$\bar{w}_i$

AMOUNT AVAILABLE (N_i)

Fig. 7. The "Economic" Case: Marginal Products Not Dependent
on Factor Supplies

If the aggregate demand function for each type of labor in
the economy were highly elastic, then we would expect to find
that the relative earnings of different types of labor would be
relatively insensitive to differences in the composition of the
labor force. (Here, and below, we assume that earnings provide
an adequate measure of the marginal productivity of the factor
in question.) Thus, by investigating the relationship between
relative earnings and relative quantities of different types of
labor, we gain insight into the elasticity of demand for labor

are not. For a review of some alternative concepts of the partial elasticity
of substitution, see Robert Solow, "Some Recent Developments in the
Theory of Production," in Murray Brown (ed.), *The Theory and Empirical
Analysis of Production*, Studies in Income and Wealth, vol. 31 (New York:
National Bureau of Economic Research, 1967), pp. 25–50. For an expres-
sion for the elasticity of demand for a factor in the multifactor case, see
Allen, *Mathematical Analysis for Economists*, pp. 507–508.

41

educated to various levels. The analysis is confined to twelve economies, both rich and poor, on which there are data on mean earnings and quantities of male labor classified by years of schooling.

I would like to estimate the elasticity of substitution, σ_{ij}, between all types of labor, L_i and L_j. This concept represents the inverse of the percentage change in the ratio of wages associated with a given percentage change in the ratio of labor quantities. More explicitly:

$$\sigma_{ij} \equiv -\frac{d(L_i/L_j)/(L_i/L_j)}{d(w_i/w_j)/(w_i/w_j)}$$

$$\equiv -\frac{d \log(L_i/L_j)}{d \log(w_i/w_j)}$$

As conventionally defined, the elasticity of substitution is a static concept and refers only to two factors in a given production process. We are considering here a case with many factors of production, only two of which are being observed explicitly in any single estimate. Moreover, the context is more aptly described as "historical" than as static; other things are not equal. Specifically, the capital stock per worker and the sectoral composition of output vary greatly among the countries in our sample. Lastly, our data refer not to a single production process, but to economy-wide aggregates. Thus, our estimated elasticity is not a parameter of some underlying technological relationship or production function, for it will reflect the combined influence of: the partial elasticity of substitution in production between L_i and L_j; the degree of complementarity or substitutability between each of the two types of labor and the excluded factors of production; and the differences in both technology and the composition of final demand.

Of course, we would like to estimate a function which would

tell us the effect of each of these above influences (taken separately) on the relative marginal products of different types of labor. This function would allow the planner to predict changes in the relative marginal productivities of labor inputs on the basis of the other elements of his plan, such as the rate of capital accumulation and changes in the composition of final demand. Although the estimates, below, of the importance of differences in the composition of final demand are a step in the right direction, we are still unable to provide a complete equation appropriate to the planning problem.

Given this unsatisfactory situation, it is the "historical" concept of the elasticity, rather than the static one, which is more appropriate to the process of planning. We would like to know the changes in relative marginal products of factors as the composition of the labor force becomes progressively better educated. The educational transformation of a labor force is an historical process in which other factors are not held constant, and which is ordinarily accompanied by substantial changes in the composition of final output. Thus, the elasticity estimated from our international cross section of countries at various stages of development is in fact the best available estimate.[3]

The data allowed the identification of three classes of workers, those with zero to seven years of schooling, called L_1, those with eight to eleven years, called L_2, and those with twelve or more years of schooling, called L_3. The basic data on factor quantities and factor prices appear in Appendix 1. The relationships

[3] To the extent that a given country's pattern of development deviates from that suggested by our cross section, of course, our historical elasticity of substitution is not quite appropriate. But it is certainly more nearly correct than a concept which holds constant all other factors, as well as the sectoral distribution of output. For evidence of a close correspondence between cross-section and time-series patterns, see Hollis B. Chenery and Lance Taylor, "Development Patterns Among Countries and Over Time" (mimeographed), Economic Development Series, Harvard University Center For International Affairs, No. 102, 1968.

43

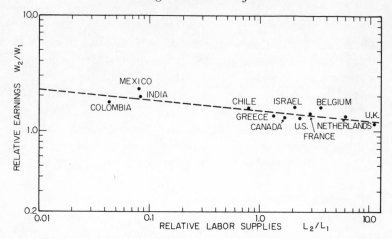

Fig. 8. Relative Earnings and Relative Labor Supplies for Labor with 8–11 and 0–7 Years of Schooling

among the data for two of the three pairs of labor are presented in Figures 8 and 9. The equations used to estimate each of the three elasticities of substitution are of the form:

$$\log \frac{w_i}{w_j} = a + b_{ij} \log \frac{L_i}{L_j}$$

In each case the composition of the labor force has been taken as the exogenous variable. This is just the reverse of the usual assumption in the case of the firm which is assumed to adjust its hiring of factors to exogenously determined factor prices. However, given the fact that the educational composition of a population is determined to a significant degree by political, cultural, and other noneconomic considerations, it seems more reasonable to represent the relative factor prices as adjusting to a factor supply situation which is (largely) exogenous.[4]

[4] Contemporary applications to schools are certainly not independent of the relative earnings of various types of labor. Given the apparent stability of relative earnings over time, the existing stocks of labor must be taken as endogenous to some extent. Thus, there is a degree of simultaneity in the relationships.

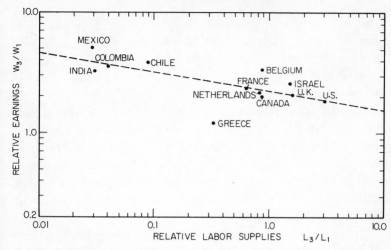

Fig. 9. Relative Earnings and Relative Labor Supplies for Labor with More than 11 and 0–7 Years of Schooling

The estimate of the elasticity of substitution is:

$$\sigma_{ij} \equiv -\frac{d \log(L_i/L_j)}{d \log(w_i/w_j)} = \frac{1}{-b_{ij}}$$

The estimated equations (with t statistics in parentheses and related information) are:

(1) $\qquad \log \dfrac{w_1}{w_2} = -.4263 - .0831 \log \dfrac{L_1}{L_2}$
$\qquad\qquad\qquad\qquad (-4.54)$

$\qquad\qquad R^2 = .6734 \qquad\qquad \sigma_{12} = 12.0$

(2) $\qquad \log \dfrac{w_1}{w_3} = -.8228 - .1552 \log \dfrac{L_1}{L_3}$
$\qquad\qquad\qquad\qquad (-3.13)$

$\qquad\qquad R^2 = .4955 \qquad\qquad \sigma_{13} = 6.4$

(3) $\qquad \log \dfrac{w_2}{w_3} = -.5486 - .0049 \log \dfrac{L_2}{L_3}$
$\qquad\qquad\qquad\qquad (-.049)$

$\qquad\qquad R^2 = .0002 \qquad\qquad \sigma_{23} = 202.0$

The first estimate implies that, when considered as part of a growth process (as represented by our cross section), a 12 percent change in the ratio of L_1 to L_2 is associated with a 1 percent change in the relative earnings. The other equations can be interpreted analogously.[5]

The estimates are consistent with the hypothesis in question, namely, that there is no strong negative relationship between relative factor prices and relative factor quantities. Although in each case the relationship is, as expected, negative, in one case the relationship is very insignificant, and in all cases the estimated elasticities are high. All are significantly greater than three at the 99 percent level of significance.[6]

The results suggest the possibility of aggregating the two best-educated categories of labor and thus allowing an estimate of the elasticity of substitution between two labor categories comprising the entire male labor force. The necessary condition for this aggregation is that the marginal rate of substitution between L_2 and L_3 be independent of the quantity of L_1, or that:

$$\frac{\partial(w_2/w_3)}{\partial\ (L_1/L)} = 0$$

[5] If we exclude positive values of b_{ij} as implausible on *a priori* grounds, the expected value of the estimate no longer corresponds to the maximum likelihood estimate reported here. Were we estimating actual production relations (rather than relations dependent on the level of other non-measured inputs and variations in output composition, as well as technology) the exclusion of positive values would seem the correct procedure. Here the case is not so clear; there is a presumption against positive values, but they cannot be definitely excluded. In any case, the expected value of the estimates of b_{12} and b_{13} would be only very slightly larger in absolute value (and the estimated elasticities correspondingly lower) were we to exclude positive values of b_{ij}. On the other hand, the exclusion of positive values of b_{23} yields an expected value of approximately $-.1$ (implying an elasticity of substitution of 10). This estimate is based on the fact that the maximum likelihood estimate of b_{23} is virtually zero. The expected value of a random normally distributed variable with mean zero and standard deviation, σ, over positive values is σ, which in this case is .1.

[6] Although there are two distinct groups of countries in the sample—India, Mexico, Colombia, and Chile and the others—the data for both groups separately are consistent with the hypothesis.

where L is the total labor force.[7] This hypothesis was tested directly by introducing L_1/L into equation (3) above. The hypothesis of no relation was accepted at any conventional level of significance.

A simple method of aggregation is suggested by the finding that the marginal rate of substitution between L_2 and L_3 is independent of the quantities of these two factors. The two best-educated categories of labor can be aggregated to form a new, synthetic factor L', where

$$L' = L_2 + L_3(w_3/w_2)$$

and w_3/w_2 is the mean ratio of wages from the international cross section. The earnings of this factor, w', are defined as

$$w' = \frac{L_2 w_2 + L_3 w_3}{L'}$$

The relationship between relative quantities and relative factor payments using this new aggregated factor, L', is estimated from:

$$(4) \qquad \log \frac{w'}{w_1} = 1.3403 - .1242 \log \frac{L'}{L_1}$$
$$(-5.165)$$

$$R^2 = .7274$$

The implied elasticity of substitution between well-educated and less-educated labor is 8.

While the magnitude of this estimate seems strongly to support the view that labor demand elasticities are high, a number of reservations should be noted. First, the data on earnings and

[7] See W. W. Leontief, "A Note on the Interrelation of Subsets of Independent Variables of a Continuous Function with Continuous First Derivatives," *Bulletin of the American Mathematical Society*, vol. 53 (1947), pp. 343–350; Leontief, "Introduction to a Theory of the Internal Structure of Functional Relationships," *Econometrica*, vol. 15 (October 1947), pp. 361–373; and Robert Solow, "The Production Function and the Theory of Capital," *Review of Economic Studies*, vol. 23, no. 2 (1955–1956), pp. 101–108.

labor quantities are subject to considerable error. The regression coefficient of the independent variable (the ratio of labor quantities) will thus be biased toward zero; the estimate of the elasticity of substitution is accordingly upward biased.[8] An upper limit to this bias can be established by making the ratio of labor quantities the dependent variable and, recalling that there are errors in both variables, regarding the estimated regression coefficient of the ratio of wages as a downward biased estimate of the elasticity of substitution itself. Reversing the order of the variables in equation (4), this procedure yielded a lower limit estimate for the elasticity of substitution between well-educated and less-educated labor of 5.9, with a standard error of 1.1.

A second serious problem arises with respect to the meaning of the schooling categories used. It is not at all clear that ten years of schooling in Indian schools represents the same level of economically relevant learning as ten years in Belgian or Mexican schools. However, I see no reason why the errors introduced through variation in educational quality should bias the estimated elasticities upward.

Third, for all the countries in the sample, my labor input measures include unemployed workers. The existence of unemployment suggests that the observed wages and quantities do not represent a market equilibrium. Because this problem is particularly severe in the poor countries, and for the lowest schooling category of labor, the estimated elasticities are biased upward. In order to calculate plausible limits for this bias, I assumed that the equilibrium quantities of L_1 in each of the four poor countries (India, Colombia, Mexico, and Chile) represented 80 percent of the observed inputs, or that the unemploy-

[8] For a survey of the errors in variable problems, see J. Johnston, *Econometric Methods* (New York: McGraw-Hill Book Company, 1963), Chap. 6. See also Maurice Halperin, "Fitting of Straight Lines and Prediction When Both Variables are Subject to Error," *Journal of the American Statistical Association*, vol. 56, no. 295 (September 1961), pp. 657–669.

ment rate among the least educated workers was 20 percent. The resulting estimate of the elasticity of substitution, from equation (4), is 7.9, or virtually the same as the original estimate.

A fourth possible objection is, to my mind, spurious. It has been contended that the absence of a strong negative relationship between labor quantities and labor payments demonstrates that wages are rigid or determined by convention. My estimates (to complete the argument) merely illustrate the implausibility of the basic assumption that wages correspond to the value of the marginal product of labor. Yet, recall that in all my estimates the direction of the relationship between relative factor quantities and payments is exactly what would be expected if labor markets were perfect, and, moreover, for all but one of the estimates, the hypothesis of no relationship is soundly rejected. Thus, far from casting doubt on the perfection of the labor market, these estimates offer mild support to the conventional microeconomic view, at least as a rough approximation.

A major remaining reservation arises from the use of cross-section, rather than time-series, estimates. Because we intend to apply these results to problems of educational development within a given country over time, we must investigate the possibility that the high elasticity apparent from the cross-section estimates is not representative of the actual historical development of any given economy. Our only available time series is for the United States, and this is limited to five observations between 1939 and 1963. We estimated equations for these United States observations, and while significance levels were low, the results are not inconsistent with the hypothesis that the actual historical elasticity in a given country is at least as high as the elasticity estimated from the cross section.[9]

[9] The implied elasticities were uniformly higher. A test of the hypothesis that the time-series and cross-section data were drawn from the same population was strongly confirmed.

In the remainder of this chapter, I shall investigate three main sources of this very high degree of labor substitutability: direct factor substitution in production, indirect substitution through changes in the composition of final demand, and the long-run high elasticity of supply of substitute factors.

SUBSTITUTION IN PRODUCTION

The production of any commodity requires the combination of various skills embodied in the labor force with other inputs such as raw materials, intermediate goods, and the plant and equipment. The possibility of substitution in production between labor with different years of schooling arises in the first place because it is not necessary for labor skills to be used in fixed proportions; there is some substitutability among skills. Second, there may also be some range in the level of education associated with each skill; years of schooling, on-the-job training, and experience are partial substitutes in the formation of most skills. Some amount of both kinds of substitution is possible in most cases.

We shall consider first the fact that a given skill may be possessed by labor of differing educational attainments. We would like an estimate of the degree of substitutability in the formation of skills between formal education and other characteristics of workers. The most important substitute for formal education in most jobs is clearly experience. The degree of substitutability between job experience and formal education undoubtedly varies from skill to skill. However, for a number of skills, the data suggest that the relationship is highly elastic. From the work of Strumilin, for example, we have data on the skill levels of St. Petersburg metalworkers (in 1919) classified by years of experience and years of schooling. Skill levels were converted to a cardinal scale, using pre-1917 wage scales. These data are presented in Figure 10 in the form of iso-skill lines.

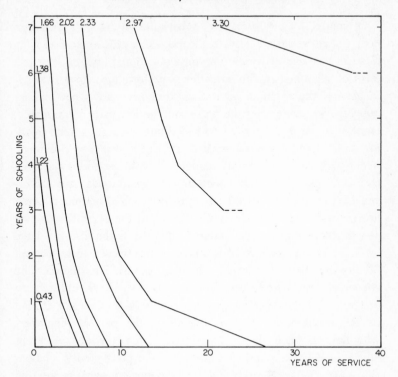

Fig. 10. Iso-Skill Functions by Years of Schooling and Experience, St. Petersburg Metalworkers, 1919

Source: Calculated from S. G. Strumilin, "The Economic Significance of National Education," in *The Economics of Education,* edited by E. A. G. Robinson & J. E. Vaizey, p. 292.

Experience and schooling appear to be good substitutes. Experienced, less-educated workers can apparently be substituted in production for better-educated, though less-experienced, individuals.[10]

[10] While one should be circumspect in generalizing this esoteric case, it is worth noting that U.S. census data on earnings, age, and years of schooling for 1959–60 suggest a similar degree of substitutability between schooling and experience. The data can be found in U.S. Census, 1960, Earnings by Education and Occupation, PC (2) 7–B.

Of course this high degree of substitutability in skill formation does not necessarily imply that each occupation will in fact be filled by workers of widely varying educational attainments. The level of schooling of the work force performing a given task is in general the result of an economic choice and is not technologically determined by the nature of the job itself. Presumably, employers weigh the added cost of filling an occupational opening with a more educated worker against the expected difference in the worker's productivity associated with his additional education. Thus, given differences in both production and factor-supply functions, we would expect to find some differences among firms and among countries with respect to the educational level of workers in a given occupation. When this is the case, we have evidence of the absence of a uniquely determined technological relationship between formal schooling and skill formation. The converse is not strictly true, however, for when we find a fairly uniform educational level among workers in a given job, it may be the result of a conscious choice on the part of employers who have at their disposal personnel from a wide variety of educational backgrounds. Of course, if the productivity relationships and the costs of hiring better-educated workers are the same within a given country, we would expect to observe a *unique* relationship between job titles and educational attainments. This relationship would, of course, be the result of each firm's optimization process and would not necessarily reflect an underlying technologically determined relation.

Some professions, of course, have unique educational requirements; medicine and law (in some countries) are probably the best examples,[11] but even jobs within these fields can apparently

---

[11] Educational "requirements" for these jobs differ significantly among countries. It should be noted that the unique relationship between schooling and occupation here derives not so much from the nature of the work or the crucial importance of education in the performance of the job as from job-entry restrictions imposed by professional organizations and enforced by the state. It would not be an exaggeration to say that a doctor is defined

be performed by people of widely varying educational attainments.

Data on the educational levels of workers in various occupations in different countries provide some insight into the degree of substitutability among workers of different levels of schooling in the performance of a given job. Most of the data refer to occupational groups so broadly defined as to make necessary considerable caution in making comparisons, and the comparability of the data in a number of other respects is also questionable. Subject to these caveats, the best data presently available suggest two conclusions: First, within a given country the distribution of workers by level of schooling within a single occupation shows a wide variation; for a representative sample of occupations in six different countries, for example, it was generally the case that considerably less than half the total workers in an occupation had attained exactly the modal years of schooling.[12] Second, any measure of central tendency in the distribution of workers by years of schooling in a given occupation shows major differences among the countries for which data are available.[13]

---

as one who has successfully completed medical school and the associated internship; the occupational title and the educational requirement are synonymous.

[12] The occupations are professional and technical workers, engineers (a subcategory of the above), clerical workers, and secretaries, stenographers, and typists (another subcategory). The countries are Argentina, Canada, Japan, Yugoslavia, England and Wales, and the U.S.A. The data are from Morris A. Horowitz, Manuel Zymelman, and Irwin L. Herrnstadt, *Manpower Requirements for Planning, an International Comparison Approach*, vol. II (Boston: Northeastern University, 1967).

[13] Additional evidence of the wide dispersion of educational attainments within an occupation relating to India, the Congo, and several European countries can be found in Herbert Parnes "The Relation of Occupation to Educational Qualification," *Planning Education for Economic and Social Development* (Paris: OECD, 1962), p. 152, and in C. A. Anderson, "Patterns and Variability in the Diffusion of Schooling," in C. A. Anderson and M. J. Bowman (eds.), *Education and Economic Development* (Chicago: Aldine, 1965), pp. 321, 322.

Although the above data are illuminating, the best information on this subject comes from the United States. Moreover, because of the existence of earnings data associated with occupation and level of education, we are able to test the hypothesis that educational requirements are placed on certain jobs. If workers have less than the "required" amount of schooling, employers find them worthless and consequently pay them very little (or do not hire them); on the other hand, education beyond the "required" years, though it may not impair one's earnings, does not enhance them either.[14] Yet the distribution of workers by level of schooling within an occupation and the relationship between schooling and earnings suggest an entirely different picture. In none of the twenty or more occupational groups and subgroups studied (including such likely candidates as civil engineers, electrical engineers, designers and draftsmen, electricians, and carpenters) did the distribution of workers and the relationship between earnings and years of schooling correspond to what would have been expected from the existence of a schooling requirement for the performance of the job.[15] While these and the above international data on the distribution of workers by educational level within occupations are little more than illustrative, they do suggest one reason for the high elasticity of substitution among labor of different levels of schooling: the absence of a unique technologically given schooling requirement for the acquisition of particular occupational skills.

Just as there are alternative methods of developing a given skill, so are there a number of ways of combining different skills

[14] This approach was suggested to me by Mark Blaug *et al., The Utilization of Educated Manpower in Industry* (London: Oliver and Boyd, 1967).

[15] The data are from the *U.S. Census, 1960,* Earnings by Occupation and Education, PC (2) 7–B. For a brief, unsystematic survey of these data, see Samuel Bowles, "The Long Run Demand for Educated Labor," Economic Development Series, No. 89, Project for Quantitative Research on Economic Development, Center for International Affairs, Harvard University, February 1968.

to produce a particular good.[16] Even if each production technology requires different labor inputs in fixed proportions, there still remains the possibility of labor substitution through the choice between skill-using techniques and those requiring few skills. Often overlooked in this respect are the various institutional choices facing an economy. Plantation or collective agriculture may economize on the use of entrepreneurial and technical skills, at least in the cultivation of some crops. Also, rigid civil service procedures serve to insure that bureaucrats will arrive at the appropriate decisions in most situations, allowing adequate performance of complicated jobs by workers with little education or administrative experience.[17]

All of the above suggests a high degree of substitutability among labor inputs in a given production process. However, direct evidence on the elasticity of substitution among labor inputs for particular sectors is fragmentary. Nonetheless, the available data suggest generally high elasticities. Marcelo Selowsky, using data from the 1/1000 sample of the U.S. Census of 1960, estimated the elasticity of substitution among various pairs of types of labor, classified by years of schooling, in fifty-nine U.S. manufacturing industries. According to his preliminary results, for all of the nine cases estimated the elasticity of substitution is significantly greater than 6 at the 95 percent signifi-

[16] Some of the best examples of this process of substitution can be found in the adaptation of the U.S. economy during World War II to the newly recruited labor force, which generally lacked industrial skills and possessed a lower average level of education than the labor force in the immediate prewar years. Among other methods used, complicated jobs were frequently subdivided into a series of relatively simple tasks, each one capable of being performed by a person with rudimentary skills.

[17] Max Weber, "On Bureaucracy," in M. M. Gerth and C. Wright Mills, *From Max Weber: Essays in Sociology* (New York: Oxford University Press, 1958), pp. 196–245. The abundance of bureaucratic red tape in many underdeveloped countries may to some degree reflect this process of substitution of decision-making rules for decision-making skills. Of course, it also reflects the capacity of colonial governments to centralize decision-making power in the hands of a few bureaucrats from the mother country.

55

cance level.[18] Further evidence is contained in a study of the education and skill composition of the labor force in U.S. agriculture by Finis Welch.[19] His preliminary results, using an equation of the form presented above, are consistent with the hypothesis of highly elastic demand functions for each type of labor.

SUBSTITUTION IN FINAL DEMAND

In addition to the possibility of substitution among labor educated to different levels within given occupations and the further possibility of substituting among skills in the production of a given product, there remains the possibility of achieving indirect substitution through variations in the composition of the economy's output. Substitution in production is complemented by substitution in final demand. Thus, a country may produce relatively little of those goods in which the comparatively scarce labor categories are intensive inputs. Because of transport costs and other trade barriers, relative domestic commodity prices are not equalized among countries. Thus, goods whose technologies are intensive in the use of particularly scarce factors are likely to be relatively expensive. For this reason we may expect that, other things being equal, countries with relatively abundant supplies of labor of one type will not only tend to export goods using large amounts of that factor, but will consume more of those goods than countries of a similar level of income.

The effect of differences in the skill-intensiveness of exports

[18] The estimated elasticities were much higher. However, given the large standard errors of his estimates, the confidence interval seems the most appropriate information to report. I am grateful to him for making these results available to me.

[19] "Education in Production," unpublished. Welch's data are from the U.S. 1960 Census.

and imports is to allow the exportation or importation of skills as embodied in internationally traded goods or services. On the other hand, substitution in consumption allows a country to "consume" its labor surplus in one area and to forego consumption of scarce embodied labor inputs. The effect in both cases is, of course, to increase the elasticity of demand for each type of labor, thereby enabling an economy to absorb large quantities of labor of one type while coping with a labor shortage in another field.[20]

The influence of a nation's relative factor endowments on the commodity composition of its exports and imports has recently been much debated, particularly with respect to the relative capital and labor intensity of commodities in foreign trade.[21] The inclusion of labor skills or human capital in the discussion is a recent development. Research by Donald Keesing strongly suggests the validity of the basic factor-endowments approach when labor skills are taken into account.[22] Using United States labor input coefficients, Keesing estimates the skill intensiveness of U.S. exports and imports, as well as those of the major European countries and Japan. His work clearly establishes that

[20] To clarify this tendency, it might be added that, using more extreme assumptions, it is possible to show that in the presence of international trade the elasticity of demand for a factor of production will be infinite, regardless of the elasticity of substitution in production. The particular assumptions and the basic argument are identical to those underlying the factor price equalization theorem. See in particular, Paul A. Samuelson, "International Factor-Price Equalization Once Again," *Economic Journal,* vol. 59 (June 1949), pp. 181–197.

[21] W. W. Leontief, "Domestic Production and Foreign Trade: the American Capital Position Reexamined," *Proceedings of the American Philosophical Society,* vol. 97, no. 4 (September 1953), pp. 332–349.

[22] Donald B. Keesing, "Labor Skills, and the Factor Content of International Trade; an Inquiry Restricted to Products of Manufacturing Industries," unpub. diss., Harvard University, 1961. For a survey of current work in this field, see Peter Kenen, "Skills, Human Capital, and Comparative Advantage," paper presented at the conference on Education and Income of the National Bureau of Economic Research, November 1968.

in terms of the relative skill requirements of commodities as produced in the United States, American exports are the most skill-intensive, followed by those of Sweden, West Germany, and Great Britain. The order of skill intensity for imports is generally the reverse of that for exports. The striking thing about Keesing's results is that trade patterns tend to reflect the general level of educational development in each country; countries rich in education are net exporters of the skills embodied in traded goods and services. This remains true even when extreme cases such as Hong Kong and India are included.

A supplementary finding of Keesing's work is that the composition of domestic final demand in the United States is considerably more skill-intensive than the composition of domestic final demand in any of the other countries studied. Apparently, the lower relative price of skill-intensive goods in countries with abundant skill supplies explains both the tendency toward skill-intensive exports and the skill-intensive composition of domestic consumption.[23]

The overall impact of variability in the composition of final demand on the degree of substitutability among labor inputs in the economy can be seen with the aid of the equations used earlier in estimating the relationship between relative factor quantities and factor payments. We have re-estimated equation (4), this time taking explicit (though crude) account of the influence of the commodity composition of output through the introduction of a variable representing the percentage of national product originating in agriculture, A/Y.[24] The resulting equation is:

---

[23] It is an interesting conjecture that in part the skill intensiveness of United States consumption is the result of a positive relationship between an individual's level of schooling and his preferences for education-intensive goods.

[24] The figures for the percentage of output coming from agriculture were taken from the UN, *Yearbook of National Accounts Statistics*, and are for

(5)
$$\log \frac{w'}{w_1} = 1.45 - .1704 \log \frac{L'}{L_1} - .0082 \frac{A}{Y}$$
$$(-5.38) \qquad (-1.969)$$

$$R^2 = .8094 \qquad\qquad \sigma = 5.9$$

The results are consistent with the explanation suggested above. The effect of holding constant the share of national product originating in agriculture is to reduce the estimated elasticity of substitution from 8.0 to 5.9. Thus the ability of an economy to vary the composition of output seems to considerably enhance the overall substitutability among labor inputs in the economy.[25]

The changes in the sectoral composition of output which normally accompany the increase in the education of the labor force as part of the normal growth process appear to be on balance education-intensive. Disaggregated cross-sectional evidence on the pattern of growth strongly supports this view. Thus if the cross-section estimates are to be given credence, as the relative abundance of educated labor increases concomitantly with per capita income, the portion of output originating in relatively education-intensive sectors increases with it. The effect of this

---

the year 1961. The definition of national product used is somewhat inconsistent. Definition of the concepts used appears in the notes to the individual country tables in the *Yearbook*.

[25] The best demonstration of the impact of changes in final output on the elasticity of demand for factors of production is found in economywide linear programming models. A number of authors have estimated the social marginal product function for a factor (using parametric programming). The fact that these functions may be highly elastic (over the relevant range), despite the assumption that the elasticity of substitution in production is zero, is direct evidence of the importance of shifts in the composition of output in the indirect substitutability among factors in the economy taken as a whole. See, for example, Michael Bruno, "A Programming Model for Israel,' in Irma Adelman and Erik Thorbecke (eds.), *The Theory and Design of Economic Development* (Baltimore: Johns Hopkins Press, 1966), pp. 327–354; and Arthur McEwan, "Development Alternatives in Pakistan: A Multisectoral and Regional Analysis of Planning Problems," unpub. diss., Harvard University, 1968.

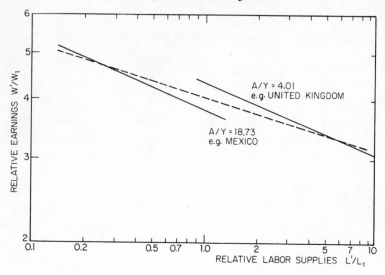

Fig. 11. The Effect of Changes in the Sectoral Composition of Output on the Demand for Educated Labor

Note: The dotted line represents equation (4). The solid lines are from equation (5). A/Y is the share of the agricultural sector in national income.

sectoral change is, of course, to shift the demand function for educated labor to the right, thus offsetting the increased supplies of labor. The process is depicted in Figure 11, where the solid lines represent the actual static relationships and the more elastic dotted line represents the longer-run expected historical relationships.[26]

We conclude that, because of the possibility of indirect substitution through changes in the composition of final demand, the educational composition of the labor force cannot be determined from the level of national income alone, even in the extreme case where each production process is characterized by fixed labor inputs per unit of output.

[26] We assume that while education intensities differ among sectors, the elasticity of substitution does not.

THE SUPPLY OF SUBSTITUTES FOR EDUCATED LABOR

Where there exist close substitutes for a factor of production and where the supply of these substitutes is elastic, the elasticity of demand for the factor itself will be high. The finding in the first section of this chapter that the elasticity of substitution between two types of labor classified by years of schooling is as high as 8 is in part attributable to the fact that skills needed in production may be acquired by a variety of means, only one of which is formal education. Learning on the job, both by formal training and through experience, is at least as important in most jobs. Employers ordinarily develop methods to generate the skills needed for the functioning of their organization—given the educational characteristics of the labor supply available for hiring in the labor market. Where the skills may be developed relatively simply and quickly outside the formal schooling system, the elasticity of supply of substitutes for educated labor will be comparatively high even in the short run.

The above data suggest that experience is a fairly good substitute for education, at least in the occupations investigated. To some extent, of course, experience represents more than learning in a simple, unsupervised, on-the-job situation. Much of the appearance of substitutability arises because the older workers have had the benefit of training and other programs designed to create the needed skills. Among methods of skill creation, training within the firm is particularly important. Training may take the form of learning on the job, informally supervised by coworkers, or it may be more formal, involving classroom work. In many craft occupations, the master-apprentice relationship is still the major source of skill creation.[27]

[27] Archibald Callaway, "Nigeria's Indigenous Education: The Apprenticeship System," *Odu*, vol. 1, no. 1 (July 1964), pp. 1–18, provides a well-documented case study of the major role of apprenticeship in the economy of a major African city.

A second major source of skill creation is the privately operated profit-motivated vocational course oriented toward the labor market. These courses are generally short and are designed to train the worker in a skill for which there is an immediate demand—typing and shorthand, sewing machine operation, auto mechanics, metalworking, Fortran programming, or whichever skills are scarce enough to induce workers to acquire them at some private cost.

A third source of supply is job switching by people who have more than one skill. When a scarcity in a particular occupation brings further remuneration, workers presently using other skills may be attracted to the field. (Movement between engineering and administrative occupations is a good example.)

In many countries, skills are available from a fourth source: foreign labor markets.[28] The international movement of labor at all skill levels and of various educational attainments ordinarily takes place between countries with similar language and cultural backgrounds, although the recent movement of labor within Europe (and from Turkey to Europe) is a major exception. Foreign and domestic labor (even when formal educational attainments are identical) are not perfect substitutes; additional costs are generally incurred in acquiring and assimilating the foreigner. Nonetheless, the international movement of labor is of considerable significance in the labor markets of many countries. Europe may be moving toward a single labor market, at least in some skills.[29] The Commonwealth nations have for many years traded in human skills at various levels. Most poor countries depend to a major degree on professional and technical personnel from more developed societies. Labor movements among poor countries are

[28] See Brinley Thomas, "The International Circulation of Human Capital," *Minerva*, Summer 1967, pp. 479–506.
[29] See Charles P. Kindleberger, *Europe's Postwar Growth and Labor Supply* (Cambridge, Mass.: Harvard University Press, 1967), pp. 171–195.

also significant.[30] In the United States, which is in many ways relatively isolated from the world economy, foreign labor markets constitute a major source of the supply of skilled labor.[31] In 1964, for example, the number of immigrant natural scientists, engineers, and doctors amounted to 3, 11, and 29 percent, respectively, of the number of first degree graduates in science, engineering, and medicine. Both the brain-drain and the brawn-drain are two-way streets; the elasticity of demand for domestic labor is increased both by the availability of foreign substitutes and by the presence of foreign employers in the market. For example, in a recent year emigrant engineers constituted a major share of the annual output of first-degree engineers in a number of European countries. West Germany lost 9 percent, Greece 20 percent, and Norway 24 percent.[32]

ALTERNATIVE MEASURES OF THE QUALITY OF THE LABOR FORCE

The choice of assumptions concerning the degree of substitutability in the market for educated labor is of course not limited to the two polar cases presented at the beginning of this chapter.

[30] Consider the present or recent importance of West African magistrates in the East African judicial profession, of Egyptian and Sudanese teachers in the Muslim areas of Africa, and of Dahomeyan civil servants throughout former French West Africa. Indian white-collar workers in East and South Africa, North Vietnamese teachers in Guinea and Mali, and Lebanese commercial personnel in West Africa are additional cases in point.

[31] Over 11 percent of the 83,000 professional scientists holding Ph.D.'s recorded in the National Register of Scientists and Technical Personnel maintained by the National Science Foundation are of foreign origin. "Foreign origin" is defined as having completed secondary school abroad; it is not synonymous with "foreign-born." The above data are from T. J. Mills, "Scientific Personnel and Professions," *The Annals of the Academy of Political and Social Science,* September 1966, pp. 33–42.

[32] Herbert Grubel and Anthony Scott, "The International Flow of Human Capital" in American Economic Association, *Proceedings,* May 1966, pp. 268–274. No year for these data is given.

While computational simplicity strongly recommends one or the other extreme assumptions, the truth, not surprisingly, falls somewhere in between. It is necessary, therefore, to assess the degree of inaccuracy involved in using either polar case, as compared with using a measure based on the actual estimated elasticities of substitution.

A sensible objective for a growth-oriented planning model of the educational sector is to maximize the amount of labor services in the economy by increasing the quality of labor. Thus, the problem of choosing the correct assumptions about the elasticity of substitution among various types of labor can be rephrased as a problem in aggregation: what is the best measure of the total labor services in an economy? Consider an economy with n types of labor, whose numbers are represented by L_i, where $i = 1 \ldots n$. How much labor does this economy have?

The first and most widely used answer is that the total amount of labor in the economy is measured by counting heads:

(6) $\qquad L = L_1 + L_2 + \ldots + L_n$

This formulation assumes that the marginal rate of substitution between any two types of labor is unity; for economic purposes all are identical. The elasticity of substitution between any two types is then necessarily infinite. This form must be rejected at the outset, as it fails to recognize the economic productivity of schooling.

A second form, which we denote L^0, recently popularized by Edward F. Denison and others in their study of the contribution of schooling to economic growth, is

(7) $\qquad L^0 = L_1 + L_2 w_2 + \ldots + L_n w_n,$

where w_i is the ratio of earnings of labor of type i to the earnings of labor, in this case type 1, an arbitrarily chosen type. It is assumed that relative earnings reflect relative marginal products.

This form of aggregation assumes an infinite elasticity of substitution between all pairs of labor; each marginal rate of substitution is unaffected by changes in the relative factor quantities. This form corresponds to polar case two outlined at the beginning of this chapter.

A third form, corresponding to the first polar case, is L^R, where

$$(8) \qquad L^R = \min \left[\frac{L_1}{a_1}, \quad \frac{L_2}{a_2}, \ldots, \frac{L_n}{a_n} \right]$$

where a_i is the minimum amount of labor of type i required to produce a given unit of outputs. The implied elasticity of substitution between each pair of labor types is zero; L^R thus arises from the assumptions used in the manpower requirements approach to planning.

A variation on the third form takes into account the fact that the relation between each type of labor input and output may not be linear, and that, moreover, the required amount of labor in an economy will depend on the productivity of the economy as well as on the level of output. (This form is introduced here less for its intrinsic interest than for its central relevance to a method of educational planning developed by Tinbergen and others, which is discussed in some detail in Chapter V.) Based on a cross-section regression study of twenty-three countries, researchers at the Netherlands Economic Institute found that[33]

$$(9) \qquad n_3 = 5.20 \ (Y \times 10^{-6})^{\ 1.202} \left(\frac{Y}{P} \right)^{-0.164}$$

and that

$$(10) \qquad n_2 = 163.67 \ (Y \times 10^{-6})^{\ 1.314} \left(\frac{Y}{P} \right)^{-0.655}$$

[33] Division of Balanced International Growth, Netherlands Economic Institute, "Financial Aspects of the Educational Expansion in Developing Regions: Some Quantitative Estimates," in Lucille Reifman (ed.), *Financing Education for Economic Growth* (Paris: OECD, 1966), Chap. 4.

where: n_2, n_3 are the estimated requirements of secondary and higher educated labor, respectively;

Y is real national income in U.S. dollars of 1957; and

$\dfrac{Y}{P}$ is national income / capita in U.S. dollars of 1957.

As a measure of the amount of labor in the economy we may use the estimate of the output made possible by the supply of labor, taking into account the (already known) actual level of output per man in the economy. If there are two types of labor, there will be two such measures, and because the functions above represent minimum labor "requirements," we must select the minimum of the two output measures in each case. (Following the Netherlands Economic Institute, we ignore the quantity of labor having less than a secondary education.) Thus we have:

$$(11) \qquad L^{R'} = \min\left[\ \frac{L_2}{a'_2} \ , \ \frac{L_3}{a'_3} \ \right]$$

where a'_2, a'_3 are computed from the above two equations by using observed labor quantities (L_2 and L_3) and income per capita, solving each equation for Y (yielding the two solutions Y_2 and Y_3) and setting $a'_2 = L_2/Y_2$, and analogously for a'_3.[34] For any given income level, the implied elasticity of substitution among labor inputs is zero.

A fourth method of aggregation embodying less restrictive assumptions concerning the elasticity of substitution can be written:

$$L^* = [d_A L_A^{-v} + d_B L_B^{-v}]^{-1/v}$$

where d_A, d_B, and v are estimated parameters and $d_A + d_B = 1$. In this case the elasticity of substitution, σ, is constant and equal

---

[34] Notice that my definition of the labor categories does not correspond exactly to those used by the Netherlands Economic Institute.

to $1/(1+v)$.[35] In order to estimate this function we make use of the assumption that relative factor prices are equal to the relative marginal production of the factors, or that

$$\frac{w_A}{w_B} = \frac{d_A}{d_B}\left[\frac{L_A}{L_B}\right]^{-1/\sigma}$$

Thus our data on relative earnings and quantities of labor of each type are sufficient to estimate the function. Because this measure incorporates an empirical estimate of the elasticity of substitution, I will use it as a criterion measure against which to evaluate the quantitative biases involved in using the assumed elasticities underlying the other methods of aggregation.

However, notice that this aggregation function refers to only two types of labor. It may be extended to include more, in the form

$$L^{**} = [d_1 L_1{}^{-v} + d_2 L_2{}^{-v} + \ldots + d_n L_n{}^{-v}]^{-1/v}$$

where $\Sigma d_i = 1$; yet this form is limited in that the partial elasticities of substitution between each pair of labor types are required to be equal.[36] The evidence from the regression equation suggests that this is not the case.[37] Thus I have adopted a two-level procedure[38] in which

[35] A function of this type is ordinarily called a constant elasticity of substitution function. For a review of recent econometric literature on the function, see Marc Nerlove, "Recent Empirical Estimates of the CES and Related Production Functions," in Brown (ed.), *The Theory and Empirical Analysis of Production*, pp. 55–122.

[36] This is the form suggested by Hirofumi Uzawa in "Production Functions with Constant Elasticities of Substitution," *Review of Economic Studies*, 29 (1962), pp. 291–299.

[37] Because of the large standard errors of the estimate of the elasticity of substitution between labor of types two and three, the hypothesis that the magnitudes were in fact identical could not be rejected at conventional levels of significance. Nonetheless, the sizable differences in the estimated coefficients suggested that there would be some loss in assuming all elasticities to be the same.

[38] See Kazuo Sato, "A Two-Level Constant Elasticity of Substitution Production Function," *Review of Economic Studies*, 34 (1967), pp. 201–218.

(12) $L^* = f[L_1, g(L_2, L_3)]$

and in which the second aggregated factor is

(13) $L' = g(L_2, L_3) = [g_2 L_2^{-k} + g_3 L_3^{-k}]^{-1/k}$

where $g_2 + g_3 = 1$. However, since we found no relationship between the ratio L_2/L_3 and w_2/w_3 [see equation (3)] we may assume that the relevant elasticity of substitution is infinite. In this case k equals -1, and the function reduces to

$$L' = g_2 L_2 + g_3 L_3,$$

which is exactly the form of aggregation used earlier in the chapter. The coefficients g_2 and g_3 represent the mean relative earnings of the two types of labor.

Thus we arrive back at the first level equation, L^*, and using the notation of our international sample, we can now write:

(14) $L^* = [d_1 L_1^{-v} + d' L'^{-v}]^{-1/v}$

Notice that our regression (4) contains the estimates of both the elasticity of substitution and the parameters d_1 and d'. Thus our final estimates for this aggregation function are:

(15) $L^* = [.7995(.3651 L_2 + .6349 L_3)^{.8806} + .2005 L_1^{.8806}]^{1/.8806}$

Measurement of the parameters of the other aggregation functions was based on the data from the international cross section. The estimated values of each labor index are expressed as a fraction of the values for the U.S. in Table 1. By dividing the aggregate labor input index by the number of workers, we have an index of labor quality. These indices are presented in Table 2, expressed as a fraction of the value of the same index for the U.S. The degree of association between the various labor quality indices is represented by the appropriate zero order correlation

Table 1. Amount of labor by country according to various labor aggregation indices,[a] expressed as a fraction of the U.S. amount

Country	L	L°	L^O	L^R	L^R'
United States	1.0000	1.0000	1.0000	1.0000	1.0000
Belgium	0.05215	0.0447	0.0417	0.0460	0.0595
Canada	0.1031	0.0867	0.0848	0.1362	0.1543
Chile	0.0400	0.0233	0.0231	0.0149	0.0170
United Kingdom	0.3504	0.2816	0.2783	0.1455	0.2017
France	0.2608	0.2081	0.2024	0.1977	0.2024
Greece	0.0530	0.0397	0.0383	0.0342	0.0393
India	2.7822	1.4118	1.4524	0.4072	0.1113
Mexico	0.1931	0.0978	0.1007	0.0282	0.0300
Netherlands	0.0697	0.0556	0.0544	0.0407	0.0535
Colombia	0.0884	0.0446	0.0462	0.0182	0.0088
Israel	0.0104	0.0096	0.0095	0.0032	0.0200

Source: See Appendix I.

[a] L is the total number of males economically active. $L°$ is calculated from equations (12)–(15). $L^O = L_1 + L_2(w_2/w_1) + L_3(w_3/w_1)$; the relative earnings are the means for the cross section of countries.

$$L^R = \min \left[\frac{L_1}{a_1} , \frac{L_2}{a_2} , \frac{L_3}{a_3} \right] ;$$

the coefficients a_1, a_2, a_3, were estimated as the mean values of L_1/Y, L_2/Y, and L_3/Y; income data are in the appendix.

$$L^{R'} = \min \left[\frac{L_2}{a'_2} , \frac{L_3}{a'_3} \right],$$

calculated from equations (9), (10), and (11).

coefficients in Table 3. It is clear from this table that, compared to the other measures, the measure based on the assumption of an infinite elasticity of substitution among labor inputs (L^O) comes extremely close to reflecting the quality of labor index as measured by the two-level function embodying the actual esti-

Table 2. The quantity of labor per worker: alternative measures of labor quality,[a] as a fraction of U.S. labor quality

Country	$Q^{\bullet}$	Q^{O}	Q^{R}	$Q^{R'}$
United States	1.0000	1.0000	1.0000	1.0000
Belgium	0.8182	0.7997	0.8827	1.1410
Canada	0.8427	0.8226	1.3213	1.4960
Chile	0.5840	0.5787	0.3737	0.4247
United Kingdom	0.8035	0.7942	0.4151	0.5754
France	0.7980	0.7761	0.7581	0.7759
Greece	0.7496	0.7222	0.6444	0.7422
India	0.5075	0.5220	0.1464	0.0400
Mexico	0.5064	0.5214	0.1462	0.1553
Netherlands	0.7977	0.7811	0.5849	0.7678
Colombia	0.5042	0.5228	0.2058	0.1000
Israel	0.9239	0.9138	1.2767	1.9272

Source: Table 1.

[a] Each measure, Q^i, for any given country, j, is equal to: $(L_j^i/L_j)/(L_{U.S.}^i/L_{U.S.})$; thus $Q_j^O = (L_j^O/L_j)/(L_{U.S.}^O/L_{U.S.})$.

mated elasticities. For all practical purposes the two indices are identical.[39]

CONCLUSION

On the basis of international cross-sectional data, we have found a high degree of substitutability in the economy between

[39] The infinite elasticity function, L^O, was calculated using mean relative wages from the sample of twelve countries. The results would not have been different had we used either U.S. or Indian relative wages. The zero order correlation among the L^O indices using different relative earnings are:

	L^O mean	L^O U.S.	L^O Indian
L^O mean	1.0	0.992	0.997
L^O U.S.		1.0	0.980
L^O Indian			1.0

Table 3(a). Zero order correlation among various labor indices

	L^*	L^O	L^R	$L^{R'}$
L^*	1.0000	0.9999	0.7842	0.5578
L^O	0.9999	1.0000	0.7745	0.5445
L^R	0.7842	0.7745	1.0000	0.9490
$L^{R'}$	0.5578	0.5445	0.9490	1.0000

labor classified by different levels of schooling. The fact that the relative earnings of different types of labor are insensitive to differences in the composition of the labor force is explained in part by the fact that most skills can be acquired in a variety of ways. Moreover, technological choices often allow for substitution in production. Thus we find that laborers of different educational levels are generally substitutable and that training and on-the-job experience, as well as capital and foreign labor, provide substitutes for education. The possibilities of substitution in production are supplemented by the indirect substitution between goods of differing education intensities in the composition of final output—both through changes in domestic consumption and through foreign trade. These findings have a number of important implications for the choice of an appropriate educational planning model.

Table 3(b). Zero order correlation among various labor quality indices

	Q^*	Q^O	Q^R	$Q^{R'}$
Q^*	1.0000	0.9973	0.8607	0.8344
Q^O	0.9973	1.0000	0.8516	0.8241
Q^R	0.8607	0.8516	1.0000	0.9651
$Q^{R'}$	0.8344	0.8241	0.9651	1.0000

First, the high degree of substitutability between different types of labor makes it impossible to derive an estimate of the number of each labor category needed solely on the basis of level of output. Even if the sectoral composition of output is known, the assumptions necessary to determine a set of labor "requirements" have been found to be implausible, and in this case there is the further problem of determining the sectoral output levels without prior knowledge of the relative factor supplies. There is no way to eliminate the element of economic choice from the educational planning problem. A planning method for education, therefore, must take into account the marginal products of each type of labor, as well as the opportunity costs of schooling.

Second, the elasticity of substitution among labor inputs is sufficiently high that we may use the assumption that labor demands are infinitely elastic as the basis for a computationally manageable "economic" approach to educational planning.

Third, the degree of substitutability in the economy is not immutable, but may be increased by a conscious policy aimed at increasing the occupational and geographical mobility of labor. Because of the short-run nature of most of the training and other programs designed to achieve this flexibility, the planning approach to these activities must differ considerably from that for the formal educational system. Yet neither planning operation can be effectively pursued in a vacuum. Educational planning for the formal school system must be supplemented by policies designed to perfect such short-run labor market adjustment mechanisms as on-the-job training and vocational courses in scarce skills.

IV · A Model for the Efficient Allocation of Resources in Education

In Chapter I, I outlined four main questions relating to the efficiency of the educational system as a producer of educated labor: 1) What amount of society's resources should be devoted to education? 2) How should the total resource use be distributed among the various types of education? 3) What educational technologies should be used? 4) What is the optimal level and the composition of the importation of labor for use within the educational system?

The model described below provides a conceptual and computational framework for answering these questions. Although the model was not designed specifically for less-developed economies, its first application was to educational planning problems in Nigeria. It since been applied to Greece and Canada.[1] In this chapter the model is described, and its operation in the Nigerian case illustrated.

We turn first to a description of the economic structure of Northern Nigerian education. (The choice of a single region in Nigeria will be explained shortly.)

---

[1] See Chapter V; also, J. R. Huntsberger, "The Efficient Allocation of Resources in Canadian Education," Project for Quantitative Research in Economic Development, Harvard University, Economic Development Report No. 103, July 1968.

THE STRUCTURE OF NORTHERN NIGERIAN EDUCATION

Before implementing the model, a number of strategic decisions concerning the geographical, educational, and temporal scope of the planning exercise had to be made. The first concerned the geographical scope. The control of enrollments and allocation of resources in Nigerian education was, at the time the model was implemented, primarily in the hands of the four regional governments. With the exception of higher education, jurisdiction over the entire system was given by the constitution to the regional governments. (Although jurisdiction over higher education was shared by the regional and federal governments, the regional governments of the universities themselves exercised most of the decision-making influence in this area.)

The model has been constructed to reflect the fact that most educational planning decisions are made in the regional capital. The policy questions asked are those facing the regional government; the constraints are defined in terms of regional resource availability. I decided to apply the model to the Northern Region because of the quality and availability of the economically relevant educational data there and because of the degree of control which the Northern government exercises over enrollments and allocation of resources.

It should be obvious from the previous chapter that not everything that can be called education need be the subject of long- or medium-range educational planning. Short, market-responsive vocational training courses, for example, may require some public supervision, but their duration and the ease with which they are expanded or contracted may render long- or medium-range planning unnecessary.

Other types of education may be the legitimate subject of educational planning, but may be such that the principles of economic efficiency cannot be sensibly applied. In some, military and medical education, for instance, a shortage may be defined in political or humanitarian terms which permit the estimation of an exact number of, say, pilots or doctors, which are "required." The nature of the requirement may be that the government has set a firm social goal of 1 doctor per 500 inhabitants, or, alternately, that it has estimated that national security will be endangered unless a given number of pilots is available. While these "requirements" should certainly be subject to the usual comparison of benefits and opportunity costs, the nature of the demand for this type of labor is sufficiently different from the demand for other categories of educated labor to warrant special treatment. Religious education may also fall into this special category.

In 1964, the educational system in Northern Nigeria consisted of 2,825 separate formal educational institutions (many with a variety of distinct courses), plus a large number of Koranic schools, in-service training programs (including military), and master-apprentice relationships.[2] (Education outside the formal schooling system has been excluded from the model.)[3] The education-producing activities used in the model are described in Table 4, which makes use of the usual input-output format to describe intra-educational flows of teachers and students. The table has been arranged so that all the student flows fall above the diagonal, while all the teacher flows fall below it.

The quantitative dimension of the system is indicated in Figure 12, which represents the stock of students enrolled in various types of schools, along with flows of newly admitted students for the year 1963.

[2] Ministry of Education, *Classes, Enrollments and Teachers in the Schools of Northern Nigeria* (Kaduna: Government Printer, 1964).
[3] In addition, lack of adequate data forced the exclusion of the Kaduna Technical Institute, a major postsecondary institution.

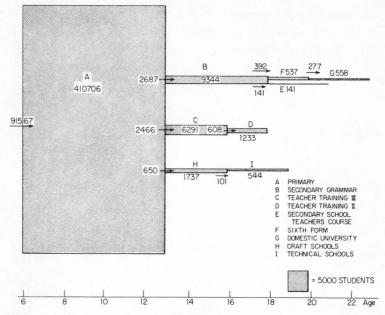

Fig. 12. Stocks and Flows in the Educational System of Northern Nigeria, 1963

Sources: Ministry of Education of Northern Nigeria, *School Statistics of Northern Nigeria* (Kaduna, 1964); Federal Ministry of Education, *Statistics of Education Nigeria 1963* (Lagos, 1965).

An outline of the content of the various courses is given below. The primary school course of studies concentrates on language skills (including literacy in English), the abilities and knowledge necessary for political participation, the development of vocational skills (chiefly "rural science" and crafts), and preparation for postprimary education. At the successful completion of the course, students are awarded the Certificate of Primary Education and may compete in the Common Entrance Examination for places in postprimary institutions. The craft schools offer a course in general secondary education which emphasizes subjects which

Table 4. The educational system of Northern Nigeria [a]

Producing sectors	Usual age of entry (years)	Duration (years) of course	Using sectors									Labor market
			1	2	3	4	5	6	7	8	9	
1. Primary school	6	7	—	S	S	S	—	—	—	—	—	L
2. Craft school	13	3	—	—	—	—	—	S	—	—	—	—
3. Grade III teacher training	13	3	T	T	—	—	S	—	S	S	—	L
4. Secondary school	13	5	—	—	—	—	—	—	S	S	—	—
5. Grade II teacher training	16	2	T	T	T	T	T	—	—	S	—	—
6. Technical training school	16	3	—	—	—	—	—	—	—	—	—	L
7. Form VI	18+	2	—	—	—	—	—	—	—	—	S	L
8. Northern Secondary Teachers College (N.S.T.C.)	18+	3	T	T	T	T	T	T	—	T	—	—
9. University	18+	3	—	—	T	T	T	T	T	T	—	L

[a] S indicates a flow of students; T indicates a flow of teachers; L indicates a flow of graduates to the labor market outside the educational sector. Some insignificant flows which have not been represented in the model have been excluded from this table.

will raise the students' level of technical trainability. The secondary grammar schools present a course in general education leading to the West African School Certificate, which is awarded on the basis of successful competition in an external examination. The elementary teacher's certificate (Grade III) course, offered at teacher-training colleges, concentrates on general subjects, with some specialization on subjects which the future teacher will endeavor to teach and some training in pedagogical technique. The course for a higher elementary teacher's certificate (Grade II) is similar except that it follows the Grade III course and proceeds at a more advanced level.[4] The technical training schools offer three-year courses in trades such as carpentry and joinery, motor mechanics, sheet-metal work, electrical installation, plumbing, and bricklaying. The Sixth Forms offer a two-year university preparatory course for secondary school graduates. Students generally specialize in three of a large number of academic disciplines chosen from the liberal arts or sciences. Successful students receive a Higher School Certificate which, if they have done well, will gain them admission to a university. Most university entrants in Nigeria hold the Higher School Certificate or its rough equivalent, the General Certificate of Education (Advanced Level). For these students the university course will normally extend over three years. Some universities allow outstanding students holding the West African School Certificate or the General Certificate of Education (Ordinary Level) to be admitted to a four-year course. The Northern Secondary School

---

[4] In 1962–63, the Grade III course was made an integral part of the Grade II course, and the intention to cease training any more Grade III teachers was expressed by the Ministry of Education. The first three years of the integrated course are to be devoted to general education, with specialization and pedagogical training being confined to the last two years. The courses are defined here as separate activities because significant numbers continue to leave at the end of three years upon receipt of the grade III certificate, and the last two years of the now integrated course still draw student inputs from the teaching force. Thus, there continues to be a definite structural discontinuity in the course.

Teachers' College (also referred to as the Higher Teacher Training College) offers specialized training in the student's prospective field and courses in pedagogical technique and the psychology of learning. Those trained in this course are expected to teach in primary schools and other postprimary institutions as well as in secondary schools. Successful students receive the Nigerian Certificate of Education (NCE).

The major remaining decision concerned the temporal scope of the model. I decided to use 1964 as a base year and to operate over an eight-year planning period. Each type of schooling is represented by a separate activity in each of the eight years.

Most approaches to educational planning make use of a longer time period. A period of eight years was chosen because there is considerable slack in the system (that is, each level enrolls only a small percentage of the output of the next lower level); for this reason a planning period only as long as the longest unbroken production process was required. A period this long allows the model to represent all the intereducational flows of students and teachers explicitly. When the model is operated on a sequential basis, as suggested below, there is little to be gained from using a longer period.

The question to which the model is addressed is: given the information available to planners in late 1963,[5] what should be the values of the instrument variables for an eight-year planning period beginning in 1964?

Before passing on to the model itself, a brief outline of the role of the educational system in the Northern Nigerian economy and a review of recent educational planning will provide a useful context in which to assess the model and its results.

That education has been at the center of most discussions of

[5] Much of the data used in the model was not actually available in 1963, but with very few exceptions it could have been. The 1964 cost data and the teacher input data presumably reflect established government policy and therefore were available in 1963.

economic planning in Northern Nigeria is not surprising, because while the educational level of the labor force is very low, the educational establishment is a major sector of the economy. In 1964 it was the largest single employer of labor with a post-primary education.[6] In addition, the educational system enrolled 476,934 students, many of whom would otherwise have joined the labor force.[7] Government expenditure on education has constituted a major portion of the total budget; during the period 1954–55 to 1962–63 recurrent expenditure by the Ministry of Education accounted for an average of 19 percent of the total. The Ministry of Education was by far the largest spending ministry in every fiscal year.[8] The proposed expenditure on educational projects in the Northern Nigeria Development Plan, 1962–68, is £19.9 million, or 21 percent of total capital expenditure. Educational expenditure is considerably larger than that on road development and agriculture—the two other significant spending categories.[9]

It is important to note that despite the large outlay of resources on the educational system, Northern Nigeria remains one of the most educationally backward areas in the world. The Ministry of Education estimated that in 1964 only 11 percent of primary school-age children were in school, and the enrollment ratios for postprimary education were much lower.[10]

[6] Federation of Nigeria, National Manpower Board, *Nigeria's High-Level Manpower,* 1963–70 (Lagos: Ministry of Information, 1964), tables 6 and 7; Ministry of Education, *Classes, Enrollments, and Teachers.*

[7] The total number of teachers employed in 1964 was 15,585. These figures do not include Amadu Bello University. See Ministry of Education, *Classes, Enrollments, and Teachers.*

[8] Government of Northern Nigeria, the Accountant General, *Report,* 1954–55 to 1962–63 (Kaduna: Government Printer).

[9] Government of Northern Nigeria, *Development Plan, 1962–1968, Project List as at 31st March 1964* (Kaduna: Government Printer, n.d).

[10] Jefferson Eastmond, "A Progress Report on Efforts to Attain the Enrollment Goals of Primary Education in Northern Nigeria" (mimeographed) (Kaduna: Ministry of Education, July 1964). This figure is computed on the basis of the 1963 census, the accuracy of which is still open to some ques-

The first effort to write a consistent and comprehensive plan for Nigeria's educational development was initiated in 1960. A group of American, British, and Nigerian educators (under the chairmanship of Sir Eric Ashby) was asked to study the post-secondary school educational system and to make recommendations for its future development. The Commission on Post-School Certificate and Higher Education in Nigeria (the Ashby Commission) asked Frederick Harbison to study Nigerian requirements for high-level manpower over the period 1960–70 to provide the quantitative basis for the commission's work. Harbison based his manpower requirements, or "targets," on information on the composition of the Nigerian labor force and economy available at the time—on assumptions concerning the future rate of growth of the economy, the levels of inputs of labor of various types into each productive sector, and the expected rate of retirement from the labor force. The Ashby Report, along with Harbison's study, became the basis of formal educational planning in Nigeria. Neither document considers the costs of the recommended pattern of enrollment.[11] It will be

---

tion. Enrollments in the first year are about 14.5 percent of the six-year-old age group. Of the two hundred territorial units listed in its 1963 *Statistical Yearbook* (Paris: UNESCO, 1964), only the following twelve exhibited lower primary school enrollment ratios: Angola, Ethiopia, Gambia, Mali, Mauritania, Niger, Somalia, Upper Volta, Afghanistan, Nepal, Saudi Arabia, and Yemen.

[11] The Ashby Report was published as *Investment in Education, the Report of the Commission on Post School Certificate and Higher Education in Nigeria* (Lagos: Ministry of Education, 1960). Professor Harbison's report is published in the same volume under the title "High Level Manpower for Nigeria's Future," pp. 50–73. In 1960, the federal government asked J. N. Archer to develop a regionally disaggregated and phased pattern of enrollments over the period 1961–1970 consistent with the Ashby recommendations, and to estimate the costs of the resulting plan. The educational plans of the Northern Nigerian government are embodied in: J. N. Archer, *Educational Development in Nigeria 1961–70, A Report on the Phasing and Cost of Educational Development on the Basis of the Ashby Commission's Report* (Lagos: Government Printer, 1961); Government of Northern Nigeria, Mini-

81

seen later that the pattern of enrollments and resource use prescribed by the model differs considerably from the educational plans of the Northern Nigerian government.

An Outline of the Model

The identification of an efficient pattern of resource allocation in education requires, first, a description of all combinations of mutually consistent enrollment levels which are feasible, given the total supply of factors. Second, we must develop a method of evaluating the desirability of each of the consistent patterns of enrollment and resource use. A standard of evaluation, or objective function, must be constructed to select the most desirable pattern of enrollment. Last, we must compare the productivity of resources in the educational system with the productivity of resources in other areas of the economy, with a view to altering the total resources available to the educational system. In this section, I outline a model designed to meet these requirements. Its central characteristic is that it deals with resource-allocation decisions in education as a problem in constrained maximization.

The model is formulated as a linear programming problem. As the technique will be unfamiliar to many readers and as its application to educational systems is somewhat unusual, a highly simplified example is presented in Appendix 2. Readers unfamiliar with linear programming may wish to consult this appendix or refer to one of the sources cited there.

We seek to determine a set of enrollments in various types of

---

stry of Education, "Estimated Capital Expenditures 1962–1967," Circular F2727/14 of 7.2.61 (mimeographed); Federation of Nigeria, *National Development Plan,* (Lagos: Government Printer, 1962), Chap. VII; and Government of Northern Nigeria, Ministry of Education, *White Paper on Educationnal Development* (Kaduna: Government Printer, 1961).

educational institutions over time in order to maximize the contribution of education to national income subject to constraints based on an educational production technology and given resource availabilities. The constraint equations define an intertemporal production possibility set for the educational system. The contribution of the educational system to future national income, which forms the maximand (or objective function), is measured by the increment in discounted lifetime earnings attributable to additional years of education.

The educational system is represented in the model as a set of production activities. Each of these processes uses a variety of inputs to transform raw materials (the uneducated) or intermediate goods (continuing students) into a producer's good. The instrument variables in the model include enrollment and resource uses at the various educational levels (primary, secondary, and so forth) in each time period. Additional instruments require discontinuous or institutional changes. Examples of the latter are choices involving new educational technologies (increased use of audiovisual equipment) or changes in the structure of the system (extending university education to a four-year course). The instrument variables have been defined to correspond to the actual policy instruments available to most governments.

In addition to the instrument variables relating to the production of specific types of education, the system is allowed to import a number of types of educated labor and to send students abroad for their education. Thus, for some types of labor the system is presented with three options: the production of labor to a given level of schooling within the country, the production of labor in foreign educational institutions, or the importation of foreign labor possessing the educational attainments in question. Other activities allow the system to recruit back into the educational sector personnel trained as teachers who are otherwise employed. In addition, four different types of school-construction activities (primary, secondary, technical, and higher) are included. Relationships between educational activities are presented as a system of intertemporal flows of students and teachers. The output of a given educational institution can be allocated to one of three tasks: to the continuation of education at a higher level; to employment as a teacher at a lower level; or to employment in the labor force outside the educational system.[12]

The constraints relate to the use of inputs supplied from outside the educational system (expenditure on education, total population in the school-going age group), as well as to endogenously supplied inputs (school construction, teachers of various types, student outputs from one educational process who appear as inputs into higher educational processes). In addition, boundary conditions limit the policy instruments to values which are judged to be politically and administratively feasible.

The method described is a sectoral model of the educational system. Production processes in the rest of the economy are not included explicitly. Thus the demand functions for the outputs of the educational system and the supply functions for the exogenously supplied educational inputs are specified prior to the operation of the model.

Educational decisions involving enrollments, resource use, and hiring of staff are generally incorporated in annual budgets or similar documents, and are made prior to the beginning of the school year, to be implemented in the course of the year. It is thus appropriate to select the year as the time unit used in the model.

In actual application the model should be operated on a year-by-year sequential basis. If the planning period is n years, the model can be operated in year 0 (the base year) and the result

---

[12] Some of the outputs will either not seek employment or will for some period of time be involuntarily unemployed.

for the years 1 . . . n computed. Only the enrollments and allocation of resources for the year 1 must be acted on at that time, so that at the end of year 1 the model can be operated once more, incorporating new information on either the production processes or the present values of the educational output. The results for years 2 . . . n + 1 can then be calculated, the values of the instrument variables for year 2 acted upon, and the process continued. Operation of the model in this manner is probably a good reflection of the actual policy-making process, which proceeds on a year-to-year basis rather than on a once-for-all basis for an entire n-year period. In addition, it allows the efficient use of new data. A further advantage is that it avoids the necessity of acting on the values of the instrument variables in the later years of the planning period, which are presumably sensitive to the somewhat arbitrary terminal conditions.

Solutions of the model yield optimal values of the instrument variables in each year of the planning period: new admissions and resource use in each type of education in each year; levels of recruitment of new inputs (foreign teachers and former domestic teachers) to the system; an efficient choice of educational techniques, including foreign as opposed to domestic university study. The solutions also generate shadow prices reflecting the productivity of resources used in the production of education.

Although the values of the instrument variables for any given solution are interesting in themselves, the results gained through parametrically programming some of the crucial elements in the model are probably more useful from the standpoint of policy-making. As will be seen, the model not only allows us to explore the production possibility set for the educational system, but also to measure the trade-off between the availability of particular inputs, on the one hand, and the values of the instrument variables, the objective function, and the shadow prices, on the other.

THE OBJECTIVE FUNCTION

The objective function represents the net economic benefits associated with the educational activities, namely, the present value of the benefits associated with the output of each level of the system in each time period minus the present value of the associated costs. Its form depends directly on the nature of demand for educated labor. The choice of a linear function in which the net benefits associated with each activity are regarded as constants, independent of the activity levels in the model, is based largely on the presumption of a highly elastic demand for educated labor established in Chapter III.

Ideally, we would like to measure the economic benefits by the increase in an individual's social marginal productivity resulting from his education. The social marginal productivity of an educational output can be described as the total effect on future national income attributable to the individual's education, taking into account his direct contribution to output, as well as any possible external effects. In the application of this model to the educational planning problems of Northern Nigeria, earnings were used as an estimate of the marginal productivity of each category of labor. While this measure is subject to a number of objections, it was thought to be the best available index.[13]

In view of the fact that each educational output has a working life extending over a number of time periods, future increases in labor productivity generated by the educational system are discounted. Ideally, the discount rate should measure the social marginal rate of substitution between present and future income. To the extent that actual government resource allocation decisions provide information about the planners' temporal prefer-

[13] A survey of reservations concerning the validity of this measure is presented in Chapter II.

ences, we might conclude that a low rate is appropriate, because all of the governments of Nigeria have devoted an unusual proportion of their resources to projects whose benefits extend over a long period of time. Education itself is probably not the best example, because, if the results presented below are to be believed, the strong governmental and popular support given to expansion in this area would have been consistent with a rather high discount rate. More persuasive evidence is afforded by the consistent willingness of the Nigerian governments to invest in projects—in various sectors, and for various durations—which are profitable only at a very low rate of discount. Studies of the social returns to capital outside the educational sector suggested a rate of 5 percent.[14]

The direct social costs associated with each activity are the present value of the annual costs per student summed over the duration of the course. The cost of one student year is the sum of the required inputs valued at their opportunity cost, that is, their social marginal productivity in the next best use, or their social marginal cost. The costs estimates exclude items of private cost such as food, accommodations, and clothing.[15]

The indirect cost element relates to the withdrawal of students from the labor force (or their retention in the educational system) for the continuation of their education. Student time is

[14] Although this figure is used throughout the chapter (except for purposes of sensitivity analysis), the choice of discount rate is necessarily somewhat arbitrary. Evidence of the low returns to investments outside the educational sector is ample. See, for example, Sayre Schatz, "The Capital Scarcity Illusion: Government Lending in Nigeria" (Mimeographed) (Ibadan: The Nigerian Institute of Social and Economic Research, 1964); Federation of Nigeria, *National Development Plan, Progress Report, 1964* (Lagos: Federal Ministry of Economic Development, 1965); Sayre Schatz, *Development Bank Lending in Nigeria, The Federal Loans Board* (Ibadan: University of Ibadan Press, 1965); and Alexander Gibb, *The Industrial Potentialities of Northern Nigeria* (London? 1963?). Of course, the fact that a number of very low return projects are included in the Nigerian plans may reveal the preference of the planners for non-income objectives rather than a low rate of time discount.

[15] The rationale for this procedure is explained in Chapter II.

valued at its opportunity cost, as estimated by the expected earnings (adjusted for unemployment and labor-force participation) of the student if he were not in school.

The net benefits coefficient associated with each activity represents the present value of the estimated stream of lifetime earnings corresponding to the type of labor produced, minus the present value of the estimated stream of lifetime earnings corresponding to the type of labor used as a student input into the production process, and minus also the present value of the direct recurrent costs. The earnings data were based on my sample survey of employment in private firms in 1965. Costs were estimated from school-by-school financial records and other data.[16] The cost of any additional school construction required by the pattern of admissions is subtracted from the total benefits. (School construction and other aspects of capacity creation will be discussed in the next section.)

The net benefits coefficient, Z_j^p, for each educational activity is

$$(1) \quad Z_j^p = Y_j^p - Y_j^p, \, - C_j^p$$

and the maximand used in the model is:

$$(2) \quad Z = \sum_{j=1}^{m} \sum_{p=1}^{n} X_j^p \, (Y_j^p - Y_j^p, \, - C_j^p) - \sum_{k=1}^{h} \sum_{p=1}^{n} V_k^p \, X_k^p$$

or

$$(3) \quad Z = \sum_{j=1}^{m} \sum_{p=1}^{n} X_j^p \, Z_j^p - \sum_{k=1}^{h} \sum_{p=1}^{n} V_k^p \, X_k^p$$

[16] The properties of the sample, the raw earnings data, and a detailed discussion of the cost estimates are presented in Samuel Bowles, "The Efficient Allocation of Resources in Education: A Planning Model With Applications to Northern Nigeria," unpub. diss., Harvard University, 1965, Chaps. 5–6.

where

X_j^p = the level of activity j in the period p (in most cases the activity level is defined in terms of the number of students admitted);

Z_j^p = the expected increase in the present value of lifetime earnings minus the present value of social costs associated with activity j in period p;

n = the number of years in the planning period;

m = the number of educational activities included in the model;

Y_j^p = the present value (discounted to year 1) of the stream of income associated with the admission of one student to activity j in period p;

$Y_{j'}^p$ = the present value of the alternative earnings-stream— namely, what would have accrued to the individual had he not received education at activity j;

C_j^p = the present value of the unit recurrent cost of operating activity j in period p;

X_k^p = the number of new student places of type k constructed in period p (k = 1 ... h); and

V_k^p = the cost of providing one additional student place of type k in period p.

The value of the function, Z, thus represents the present value of the contribution of the educational system to future national income.[17]

[17] According to the conventions of national income accounting, the value of output in the educational sector is measured by the total expenditure on education. In this model, on the other hand, education is regarded as an intermediate good rather than as a final commodity. Thus, in this case the contribution of education to national income is the market measure of the value of output *minus* direct expenditure and imputed costs.

The objective function is additive both in the strict mathematical sense and more directly in that the net benefits of educating an individual from first grade through any given level of school are the sum of the net benefits of the educational activities required to reach that level. For example, if we let the subscripts 1 and 2 refer to primary and secondary schools, respectively, and ignore dropouts, capital costs, and the temporal sequence of events, the net benefits of schooling from the first year of primary school through the end of secondary school are:

(4) $Z_1 + Z_2 = (Y_2 - Y_1 - C_2) + (Y_1 - Y_0 - C_1)$

or

(5) $Z_1 + Z_2 = Y_2 - Y_0 - C_2 - C_1$

Thus the value of output from one activity becomes part of the imputed cost of another.

The coefficients of the objective function have been adjusted to take account of the fact that not every student successfully completes his studies and that graduates and dropouts alike may either not seek work or not find work for part of the time. Because of the differences in labor-force participation rates between the sexes, the outputs of some levels have been disaggregated by sex as well as by the year of leaving the system. Table 5 presents the product mix categorized by general type of output (pass, fail, dropout) and adjusted for the relatively low labor-force participation of female students and for the unemployment of primary school graduates. It was conservatively assumed that primary school dropouts are no more productive than those who never attended school and, further, that the unemployment rate among primary school graduates participating in the labor force would be 100 percent for the first full year after graduation and 10 percent thereafter.[18]

[18] The existence of unemployment among primary school leavers is probably best understood as part of a short-term process whereby young people

The effect of wastage on the input structure is relatively minor. In the present institutional setup, the teaching inputs are proportional not to the number of students actually attending at any given moment but to the number of students originally admitted. This is a reflection of the fact that classes are organized in groups of a given number of students; as that number falls, the number of classes remains constant, thus not relieving any of the teachers. The only major reduction in cost occasioned by the dropouts is in the recurrent costs for noneducational purposes (food, and so forth).[19]

The resulting net benefits coefficients and some of the underlying data are presented in Table 6. A summary of the formal structure of the model is presented in Appendix 3.

A number of objections can be raised against the use of this objective function: the relation between wages and marginal products may be highly distorted; the effects of future changes in the economy, particularly growth, are ignored; the choice of a discount rate is arbitrary; and earnings differences may exaggerate the unique effects of education. Perhaps the most serious objection is that a linear maximand is inappropriate because the net benefits associated with each activity depend on the level of that activity, as well as on the level of the other activities in the model. To the extent to which this problem arises because the

---

adjust both their expectations concerning job status and their supply price downward to conform to the market. In this setting, it does not reflect a permanent surplus of this type of labor. For an elaboration of a similar view of unemployment among educated labor, see Mark Blaug, P. R. G. Layard, and M. Woodhall, "The Causes of Educated Unemployment in India," unpub. manuscript, 1968. For a view of the problem of unemployment of primary school graduates in Nigeria, see Archibald Callaway, "Unemployment Among African School Leavers," *Journal of Modern African Studies*, vol. 1, no. 3 (1963).

[19] Wastage may occasion a minor reduction in building and equipment costs, but this is not likely to be quantitatively significant. Failure to adjust the total social cost to take account of the reduction occasioned by wastage may thus represent a slight overestimate of the costs of education.

Table 5. The educational product mix, Northern Nigeria

Level of schooling	Type of output	Years of course completed	Percent of total intake expected to complete the number of years indicated and to find employment [a]
Uneducated [b]			91.0
Primary school	Leaver	6 or 7	58.5
	Dropout	1 . . . 5	13.1
Craft school	Leaver	3	96.0
	Dropout	2 or 1	4.0
Grade III teacher training	Pass	3	59.9
	Fail	3	33.7
	Dropout	1, 2	
Secondary school	Pass	5	48.6
	Fail, Class IV	4, 5	38.6
Grade II teacher training	Pass	2	37.3
	Fail, Dropout	1, 2	57.7
Technical training school	Pass	3	100.0
Form VI	Pass	2	57.5
	Fail	2	42.5
Northern Secondary Teachers College	Pass	3	50.7
	Fail, Dropout	1 . . . 3	49.3
University	Graduate	3, 4	78.9
	Dropout	1, 2, 3	21.1

[a] Figures in this column are derived from the wastage and failure rates and the labor force participation and unemployment rates presented in Appendix 5.3 of Samuel Bowles, "The Efficient Allocation of Resources in Education: A Planning Model with Applications to Northern Nigeria," unpublished Ph.D. dissertation, Harvard University, 1965.

[b] In view of the fact that some of the uneducated who attend primary school would not have sought employment on the labor market had they remained outside the educational system, the lifetime earnings-stream foregone by the decision to transform an uneducated person into a primary school leaver must be adjusted downwards. This figure of 91 percent represents the labor force participation rate for the uneducated (aged 13 and above) and is based on the assumption that all males and 70 percent of the females participate in the labor force. This figure may be somewhat too high and may therefore understate the benefits stream associated with primary education. As the earnings-stream of this group must be compared with that of those attending primary school, the sex composition of the uneducated is made roughly equivalent; that is, 30 percent are females.

Table 6. The present value of net benefits associated with various educational activities in Northern Nigeria, 1964[a] (adjusted for wastage, failures, labor force participation and unemployment).

Activity (1)	Present value of lifetime earnings[b] Y_j (2)	Present value of lifetime earnings foregone[c] Y_j' (3)	Increment in present value of earnings (2) − (3) (4)	Present value of direct recurrent social costs[d] C_j (5)	Present value of net benefits (2) − (3) − (5) Z_j (6)	Ratio of present values of increment in earnings to direct costs[e] (4)/(5) (7)
Primary school	1,659	611	1,048	61	987	16.9
Secondary school	4,592	2,910	1,682	426	1,256	3.9
Technical training school	4,337	2,713	1,624	733	891	2.1
Form VI	7,460	7,356	104	317	−213	0.3
University	20,559	9,130	11,429	892	10,537	8.5
University abroad	20,559	9,130	11,429	1,730	9,699	6.6

Note: All figures are in £'s and are based on a 5 percent discount rate.

[a] Net benefits coefficients for activities making no direct deliveries to the labor market (i.e., craft schools, which serve as feeders for technical training schools, plus the three types of teacher training) do not appear in this table. The demand for the outputs of these activities is derived endogenously from the admissions levels in the optimal solution. The net benefits coefficients in this table refer only to activities in the base year, 1964.

[b] Based on a sample survey of private firms in Northern Nigeria. See Samuel Bowles, "The Efficient Allocation of Resources in Education: A Planning Model with Applications to Northern Nigeria," unpublished Ph.D. dissertation, Harvard University, 1965.

[c] The present value of income foregone is the discounted lifetime earnings-stream of an individual who enters the labor force with the prerequisites for admission to level j. Thus, the alternative earnings-stream from Form VI is the stream accruing to those who have passed the West African School Certificate, not the composite secondary school stream adjusted for failures, dropouts, etc.

[d] Total costs, including maintenance, minus "private costs," namely, food and clothing. Cost figures are from the files of the Ministry of Education, Kaduna, Nigeria. See Samuel Bowles, ibid.

[e] The ratios in Column 7 are not used in the operation of the model. They are presented here merely for reference.

earnings of each type of labor depend upon the relative amounts of labor available in the economy, the material in the previous chapter suggests that the problem is not particularly serious except where changes in the educational composition of the labor force are very substantial.[20] Where the problem arises because of an inelastic supply function for some inputs into the educational process, we have artificially introduced a rising supply price for these inputs.

It is possible, of course, that if the average ability of the student is inversely related to the level of admissions, the increase in productivity associated with schooling may not be independent of the pattern of enrollments. A number of reasons for regarding this problem as of relatively minor significance are presented in Appendix 4.

However, the choice of a linear maximand was not motivated primarily by a belief in its exact correspondence to reality. Computational feasibility was a contributing factor. Because the lifetime earnings of a particular type of labor appear as lifetime foregone earnings in the objective function coefficient of other activities, and because of the intertemporal nature of the problem, the introduction of inelastic demand functions for each type of labor would render the objective function not only nonlinear but, more serious from a computational standpoint, nonseparable.

No direct test of the importance of the shortcomings of the objective function is available; however, tests of the sensitivity of the results of the model to alternative assumptions indicate that the policy prescriptions derived from the model are relatively insensitive to plausible changes in the assumptions or the underlying data. While this result is encouraging, it should not be

[20] However, the results from the three-factor model in Chapter III cannot be extended directly to this planning model, which produces five distinct types of labor for use in the economy.

interpreted as a general characteristic of the model. The importance of these objections is an empirical question which must be tested in each application of the model.

Factor Supply and Capacity Creation

The two main factors supplied from outside the system are the total social expenditure on education and the number of six-year-old children. Estimates of the availability of six-year-olds based on the best available demographic data indicate that under no conditions could primary education expand so rapidly over the period as to exhaust the supply of children. Total social expenditure on education is regarded as a variable rather than as a parameter in the model. In a later section, the constraint on the total social expenditure is varied over a wide range to allow estimation of the effects of various levels of expenditure on optimal enrollments, the pattern of resource use, the total contribution to future national income, and the shadow prices of resources used by the educational system.

The supply of teachers and students available for further schooling depends to some extent on educational decisions made prior to the planning period, as embodied in the existing stock of teachers and students in school in the base year. The surviving stocks of teachers and outputs of students admitted prior to the base year are estimated using various retirement rates for different types of teachers and the appropriate dropout and failure rates for each type of student.

Thus far we have made the usual linear programming assumption that inputs are available at constant cost up to some level, beyond which they are not available at any price. An attempt has been made to modify this somewhat extreme requirement by constructing supply functions which reflect the rising supply price of the factor. This was done by allowing the system to use a new activity which recruits the input at some additional cost. The supply functions for two types of teachers, each of which may be hired locally or imported, are depicted in Figure 13. The vertical distance between the first and second segment of each function is the cost of importing the teacher, namely, transport and other payments in addition to salary. The cost of using the teacher (salary) is charged directly to the schooling activity hiring the teacher. The lengths of the horizontal line segments in Figure 13 are determined by the available domestic supply and the maximum limit on importation. Similar activities allowing the recruitment of former teachers into the school system have been constructed. The introduction of these activities for the recruitment of Grade II and Grade III teachers (used largely in primary schools) has the effect of adding a step to the present supply functions and thus reflecting the rising supply price of these inputs.

The cost associated with recruiting former teachers is not the necessary increment in salary, or the average cost, but rather the marginal cost of hiring. The marginal cost reflects the effect of additional hiring on total costs, assuming that newly recruited domestic teachers and those already in the system must be paid the same. The system-wide increment is, of course, intended to reflect the increasing opportunity cost of using teachers, as more and more are recruited from other increasingly high productivity jobs outside the educational system.

The fundamental difference between the recruitment of foreign as opposed to domestic teachers is that teachers from abroad are considered to be noncompeting vis-à-vis Nigerians with the same qualifications: thus, what amounts to two separate salary scales exists. Hiring a foreign teacher with a university degree, for example, does not affect the opportunity cost (or the money

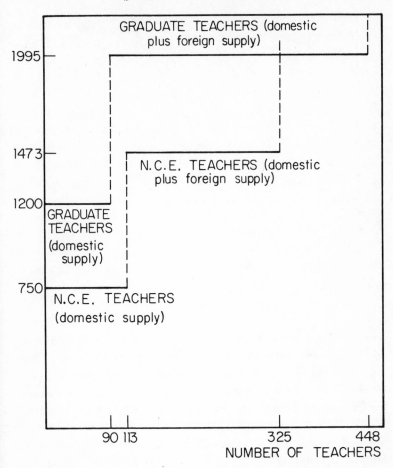

Fig. 13. Marginal Factor Cost Functions (in £'s) for Graduate Teachers and Nigerian Certificate of Education Teachers, 1965

Note: Graduate teachers refer to those holding a university degree. Nigerian Certificate of Education (N.C.E.) teachers and their foreign equivalents have completed eight years of postprimary education, the last three (for Nigerians) in the Northern Secondary Teachers College (N.S.T.C.).

97

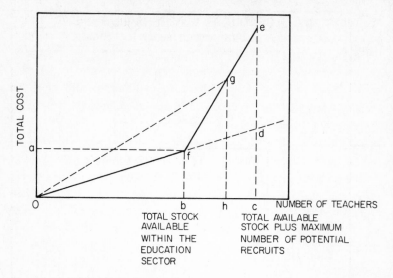

Fig. 14. Total Cost Function of Teachers Illustrating the Marginal
and Average Costs of Recruitment

cost, for that matter) of using a similarly qualified Nigerian
within the educational system. The distinction can be best
illustrated in Figure 14, which presents two different interpre-
tations of the aggregate supply function for teachers, represented
by Ofge. First considering the hiring of any type of teachers,
a0/0b is the average and marginal cost of hiring each teacher
originally within the educational system. When we are considering the recruitment of foreign teachers, ed/bc is the average increment in salary (and other costs) required to induce foreign
teachers to accept employment in Northern Nigeria. In this case
it is assumed that Nigerian teachers continue to be paid at their
lower cost, a0/0b.

On the other hand, when we consider the supply function for
Nigerian former teachers recruited back into education, Figure
14 must be interpreted differently. In this case, the function Ofge

is a single supply function. Thus ed/bc is the marginal cost of hiring new teachers. At any point on the function, say, g, the average salary paid to all teachers is gh/Oh.

The main source of endogenous capacity creation is teacher training and school construction. Four different categories of teachers are defined: Grade III teachers; Grade II teachers; Nigerian Certificate of Education teachers; and university graduates.

The first three are produced in institutions which specialize in teacher training and which require a somewhat complicated treatment in the model. Because the system not only enrolls students who will ultimately join the labor force outside education, but also devotes a considerable portion of its resources to additional capacity creation, we are faced with a problem. The demand for teachers is endogenous to the model; it is derived from the enrollment levels in the educational system, which are in turn derived from estimates of the economywide demand for educated labor. Thus we cannot directly specify a benefits-stream for teacher training. Yet, if we count only the cost (but not the benefits) of teacher training in the objective function we will in fact be double counting, as the annual cost of hiring a teacher of given qualifications is to some extent a reflection of the cost of production. Thus we would take account of the cost of teacher training once, as they are being trained, and once again, as they are used in the schools.

An equally serious problem arises because in most cases the full cost of training is incurred during the planning horizon, whereas the teacher's productive life extends far beyond it. Thus, even if we were not double counting costs during the planning period, we would be ignoring a major part of the benefits of teacher training unless we could evaluate the social marginal productivity of teachers in the years beyond the planning horizon. The solution adopted here is to charge the activities which use teachers the annual salary of the teacher and to place no cost or benefit in the objective function for the teacher-training activities. Hypothetically, the educational system *rents* the teachers from society at large; we thus abstract from both the costs and the benefits of the enlarged terminal stock of teachers. (A somewhat different approach to this problem is used in Chapter V in the application of the model to the Greek educational system.)

A related problem concerns physical capacity, or school buildings. Four distinct types of physical capacity are defined in the model (primary, secondary, technical, and higher), along with four school-construction activities for each of the eight years in the planning period.[21] Existing capacity is defined by the number of student places available in 1964. As the recurrent cost figures associated with each schooling activity include a maintenance charge, it is assumed that this stock and any newly created capacity are maintained. Thus the only charge to the building activities is an interest charge extending from the year of construction to the end of the planning horizon. If C_k is the cost per student place of a building of type k, and i is both the interest rate and the discount rate, the cost, V_k^p, of operating building activity k in year p of the planning period is

$$(6) \quad V_k^p \quad \sum_{t=p} i \, C_k \, (1+i)^{-t+1}$$

T is the last year of the planning horizon. There is no interest charge on buildings constructed prior to the planning period; the opportunity cost of these buildings is zero.[22] The maintenance

[21] Secondary includes all types of teacher training as well as secondary grammar and Form VI schools. Technical includes craft schools and technical training schools.

[22] In an earlier version of the model, I applied an interest charge to all buildings on the grounds that at the margin there were alternative uses of these structures. I now believe that this led me to overstate the real capital costs in the system.

charge is applied to both old and new buildings when in use. The interest charge applies to new buildings whether in use or not. Building costs per student place, C_k, and V_k^p for year 1 (1964) appear in Table 7. The underlying data are from architectural plans and cost estimates for new school construction.

Table 7. Annual capital costs per student place and building costs per student place (£) in Northern Nigeria, 1964

Type of building	Total cost per student place (C_k) [a]	Total costs charged for building one student place [b]
Primary	18.8	6.3
Secondary	274.7	93.0
Technical	575.1	195.0
Higher	3,264.8	1,107.0

[a] See Samuel Bowles, "The Efficient Allocation of Resources in Education: A Planning Model with Applications to Northern Nigeria," unpublished Ph.D. dissertation, Harvard University, 1965.

[b] See text.

THE CONSTRAINTS

The set of feasible enrollment levels depends on both the factor supplies available to the educational system and the production functions for the individual educational processes. We would like to know the structural relationships between inputs into the schools and educational outputs—if possible, measured in terms of the economic characteristics of those who complete the course. As was discussed in Chapter II, our knowledge of the underlying educational production functions is at present rudimentary. For this reason we have chosen to use "average" production relations, reflecting the input-output relationships most likely to be observed. They are in no way intended to represent the underlying "technological" relationship between school inputs and outputs.

For any level of education, j, in period p, the production function can be written:

$$(7) \quad X_j^p = \min_{i,t} \left[\frac{X_{ij}^t}{a_{ij}^t} \right] \quad \text{for} \quad \begin{matrix} j = 1 \ldots m; \\ i = 1 \ldots m + q; \text{ and} \\ t = p \ldots p + s_j - 1 \end{matrix}$$

where:

X_j^p = the number of students admitted at level j in period p;

X_{ij}^t = the amount of input i devoted to activity j in period t;

a_{ij}^t = the amount of input i required to accommodate one student in activity j in year t; [23]

m = the number of types of education considered in the model;

q = the number of factors supplied from outside the educational system; and

s_j = the number of years in course j.

The production function states that admissions, X_j^p, cannot exceed the value of the smallest ratio of total inputs (X_{ij}^t) to the relevant input coefficient (a_{ij}^t).

The a_{ij}^t coefficients referring to inputs produced by the education system itself represent teacher-student ratios for each of the types of teachers used in the model and student-input ratios.

[23] Many of the a_{ij}^t coefficients are zero.

102

The latter refer to the minimum number of graduates from level i required to admit one student to level j in time t. If level i is the "feeder" for level j, then the relevant input coefficient is 1.[24] The a_{ij}^t coefficients for inputs supplied from outside the system represent the marginal resource requirements per student. Other input coefficients refer to building and equipment requirements per student. Note that the input coefficients (a_{ij}^t) have a time superscript to indicate the possibility of technological change in the production of education.

Outputs of educational activities appear in the system of constraint equations as negative inputs, and are computed on the basis of the total original student input multiplied by the fraction of the original students who can be expected to fall into each output category, namely, dropouts, failures, and graduates. School construction activities produce student places, defined also as negative inputs.

The choice of a production technology embodying constant returns to scale is dictated in part by the institutional setting in which decisions are made. Economies of scale may exist in the individual (school) production processes, but, if expansion of enrollment is likely to take place by duplicating schools of the existing size, the correct aggregate function is one characterized by constant returns to scale. For example, a detailed study of architectural specifications and cost estimates indicated that costs

[24] In one case (Northern Secondary Teachers College), the students inputs are of two different types, secondary school leavers and Grade II teachers. In this case, the student input coefficients relating to these students have been set at fractional values representing the student input structure of this particular institution. A more flexible procedure would have been to define two distinct activities, identical except for the source of the student intake. In this case, the student input composition of the school in question would have been determined by the optimization process itself. The small size of the affected activity and considerations of the size of the model, however, recommended the simpler, more restrictive procedure.

per student place at all postsecondary institutions fell as the total enrollment per institution increased. Yet the evidence of recent years suggests that enrollment increases are accommodated largely by increasing the number of schools rather than by increasing the average size of institution. There was no evidence of decreasing unit costs with respect to other inputs.[25] Thus while the relevant input concept is marginal rather than average cost, there were good grounds for assuming that the two quantities coincided. In university education, however, there are significant indivisibilities and fixed costs, and, consequently, a major divergence between average and marginal costs. In the case of university education it was judged likely that additional enrollments would be accommodated in existing institutions with less than proportional changes in existing plant and equipment. In these cases marginal costs and input requirements (over the relevant range) were estimated and used in the operation of the model.[26]

The matrix of a_{ij}^t's, along with the output coefficients, is an intertemporal input-output system representing the intraeducational flow of teachers and continuing students along with the inputs of exogenous (primary) factors. It closely resembles an intertemporal input-output system for an entire economy with the major exception that the educational production processes are extremely time-consuming.

[25] Conflicting evidence on the presence of economies of scale in the production of United States secondary education is contained in James S. Coleman, *et al.*, *Equality of Educational Opportunity* (Washington: Office of Education, 1966), Chap. 3; John Riew, "Economies of Scale in High School Organization," *Review of Economics and Statistics*, vol. 48, no. 3 (August 1966), pp. 280–287; and E. Cohn, "Economies of Scale in Iowa Public High School Operations" (mimeographed), Department of Economics, Iowa State University, November 27, 1967.

[26] In future extensions of this model, particularly in the field of higher education, the application of integer programming should be considered.

The input coefficients relating to Northern Nigeria were estimated on the basis of historical and present data on teacher-student ratios (for a number of different types of teachers) and other input data. Time series of teacher-student ratios for each of the four types of teachers were used as the basis for the projection of future changes in the teacher input coefficients.[27] In most cases, the movements of the coefficients indicates a significant improvement in the quality of the staff, namely a substitution over time of relatively well-trained teachers for less-trained teachers. An illustration of this process of technological change can be seen in Figure 15, which presents the estimated values of teacher input coefficients for primary schools over the years 1964 to 1971.

Recall that there are three possible uses for the output of any activity: pursuit of further education in the system, employment as a teacher in the system, or employment in the labor force outside the system. These can be referred to as use as an intermediate good, use for capacity creation, and deliveries for final demand. The total requirements within the educational system for labor of a given type thus depend on the levels of the activities which use it as a teacher or as a student input. The total availability of individuals with each qualification is given by the numbers surviving from the base period plus the amount produced within the system or recruited from outside. The constraint equations insure that the number of teachers and continuing students required by a solution does not exceed the number available.[28]

Thus for inputs which are defined as a stock and which are generated within the educational system (namely, teachers):

[27] The time-series regressions and other data underlying these estimates are discussed in Bowles, "The Efficient Allocation of Resources in Education," Chap. 5.

[28] The complete set of equations appears in Appendix 3.

$$(8) \sum_{j=1}^{m} \sum_{p=t+1-s_j}^{t} a_{ij}^{t} X_j^{p} - \sum_{p=1}^{t-s_i} g_i X_i^{p} - X_{i*}^{t} \leq B_i^{1} (1 - d_i)^{t-1}$$

where:

X_j^{p} = the number of students admitted to level j in period p: $j = 1 \ldots m$, $p = 1 \ldots n$;

X_{i*}^{t} = the imports of type i in period t;

a_{ij}^{t} = the minimum input of resource i in period t required to accommodate one student in activity j; $t = 1 \ldots n$, $j = 1 \ldots m$, $i = 1 \ldots m + q$, where q equals the number of exogenously supplied inputs;

B_i^{t} = the amount of resource i available to the system in time t;

s_j = the length of course j in years (similarly defined for s_i);

d_i = the expected annual rate of retirement from the teaching force for teachers of type i; and

g_j = the fraction of the total admissions to activity X_j expected to complete the course successfully.

The first term of the expression represents the total enrollments in activity X_j at time t, multiplied by the required input of teachers of type i per student in activity j, summed over all the m activities. The second term is the total output, since the beginning of the planning period, of the teacher-training activity-producing resource (i), adjusted for failures and dropouts. The third term is the total importation or recruitment of teachers of type i from outside the educational system in time t. The

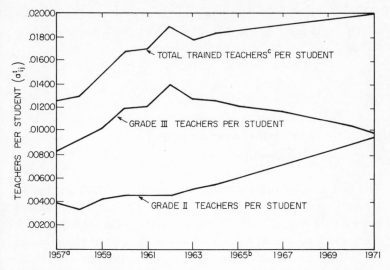

Fig. 15. Historical and Projected Technological Change in the
Production of Northern Nigerian Primary Education

[a] Values for 1957–1964 are actual.
[b] Values for 1965–1971 are projected.
[c] Grade III and Grade II teachers have completed 3 and 5 years of post-primary education respectively. Teachers with less than Grade III qualifications are not represented here, although they still occupy an important place among the primary school staff.

right-hand-side term is the total stock of type i teachers in the system in the first year of the planning period who have remained (those who have not retired) up to year t. Thus, the above set of equations requires that total use of type i teachers not exceed the available supply for each type of teacher in each year of the planning period.

There are thirty-two constraints of this type corresponding to one per year for the following inputs: Grade III teachers; Grade II teachers; Nigerian Certificates of Education teachers; and university graduate teachers.

Further, we have constraints on the use of students, inputs which are defined in flow terms and which are generated within the system.

$$(9) \; \sum_{j=1}^{m} a_{ij}^{t} \; X_{j}^{t} - g_{i} \; X_{i}^{t-s_{i}} \leq 0$$

$$a_{ij}^{t} = 1 \text{ if i is the feeder school for j}$$
$$= 0 \text{ otherwise}$$

The first term of this constraint represents the total number of students with qualifications i required as inputs into educational processes in time t, while the second term is the total output of the activity producing these students at the end of the previous year. This set of equations thus requires that the intake of students into a given type of school in time t not exceed the previous year's output of students with the prerequisite qualifications for entry.

There are thirty-two of these constraints corresponding to one per year for the following inputs: primary school leavers; craft school leavers; secondary school leavers; and Form VI leavers.

Similarly, the total number of available student places depends on the initial stock of buildings and new construction undertaken during the planning period. In this case, the constraint requires that the total enrollment in each type of school not exceed the available student places.

The constraints on the use of exogenously supplied resources refer to such inputs as primary-school-age population and total social expenditure on education, and require that the total use of each resource not exceed the exogenously specified supply.

In addition to the resource constraints, boundary conditions, reflecting the political difficulties involved in any drastic reduction in enrollments and the administrative obstacles to any very rapid increase, are imposed on the instrument variables. On the basis of recent movements in enrollments and an assessment of the political and administrative limitations facing the government, each activity was constrained to a value between .7 and 1.3 of the value of the previous year.[29]

Additional constraints are required by the finiteness of the planning horizon and by the fact that many of the activities in the model (producing either intermediate goods or capacity) do not deliver to final demand and thus produce no direct benefits. In the absence of any terminal conditions, these activities would not operate during the last few years of the planning period. The system could consume its capital by using up its goods in process (students continuing their education) and by not replenishing the teachers who retire. In order to provide for postterminal educational growth roughly conforming to that prescribed in the planning period, we have set the relevant activities in the preterminal years at levels sufficient to maintain the rate of growth observed during the period. Chapter V provides a more complete discussion and an alternative specification of the terminal conditions).

Before considering the actual solutions, it should be pointed out that the production side of the model as represented by the constraint equations alone is sufficient to generate alternative patterns of enrollment which are both internally consistent and which do not violate the exogenously specified resource constraints. The intertemporal production possibility set for the educational system could easily be merged with a larger optimizing model for the entire economy. Moreover, the inverse of the matrix of input and output coefficients is a convenient summary of the available educational technologies and allows the computation of the direct and indirect input requirements for a

[29] For a variety of reasons, the lower limit was not imposed on technical education or on teacher training.

unit of final delivery of each type of labor to the labor force. Using the inverse, we can easily calculate the direct and indirect school enrollments and costs necessary to satisfy a particular set of labor requirements. Thus we can solve a number of planning problems without reference to the discounted future earnings-stream attributable to education. The objective function provides one (but not by any means the only) method of selecting a desirable solution from the multitude of feasible solutions.

OPTIMAL ENROLLMENTS AND RESOURCE ALLOCATION WITHIN THE EDUCATIONAL SECTOR

Only a small portion of the results generated by the model will be discussed below; emphasis will be on the insights into concrete policy problems which can be gained through the aid of this approach to educational planning. (Well over a hundred solutions of the model have been computed, using alternative assumptions concerning policy, technology, and future demands for educated labor.)

This section will present some of the results concerning enrollments in the various types of schools. The following three sections will deal with the choice of techniques, the optimal total resource use by the educational system, and the pattern of importation of educated labor.

Solutions to the model yield values for the instrument variables relating to the admission of students to each type of school in each year of the planning period. Table 8 presents summaries of total admissions over the eight-year period, compared with roughly analogous data from the current Nigerian plans.

Most striking in many respects is the behavior of primary education. The present Northern Nigerian educational plans call for a very gradual increase in primary school enrollments accom-

Table 8. Cumulative admissions from current Northern Nigerian plans
and the solution of the model, 1964–1971

Activity	Current Nigerian plans [a]	Solution of model
Primary school	816,000	1,183,324
Craft school	[b]	0
Grade III teacher training	22,800	38,572
Secondary school	51,900	5,654
Grade II teacher training	17,230	29,287
Technical training school	[b]	0
Form VI	2,560	5,002
Northern Secondary Teachers College	1,335	2,981
University	3,500	2,608
University abroad	1,000	0

[a] Based on the Archer Report, except for the domestic university enrollments, which are estimated from the Federal Ministry of Information, *Report of National Universities Commission* (Apapa: Nigerian National Press, Ltd., 1963), p. 35. See Appendix 7.2 of Samuel Bowles, "The Efficient Allocation of Resources: A Planning Model with Applications to Northern Nigeria," unpub. diss., Harvard University, 1965.

[b] I was unable to find a quantitative estimate of the planned expansion of technical training and craft schools, although all sources suggest that the rate of growth here is planned to exceed that in most other parts of the system.

panied by gradual increases in the associated teacher-training institutions, as indicated in Figure 16.[30]

The model, using much of the same data, yields a radically different pattern of growth, also shown in Figure 16.[31] The rapid

[30] Given the planned upgrading of the primary school teaching staffs, the admission levels in current government plans are inconsistent. The demands for Grade II and Grade III teachers derived from the planned primary school admissions in the plan's early years appear to be considerably in excess of current availabilities plus planned outputs. Only a major program of recruitment of former teachers could render the existing plans feasible.

[31] The planned admissions figures represent the outcome of a comprehensive planning process which took into account a number of noneconomic aspects of the problem not considered in this model. Thus the figures are not strictly comparable.

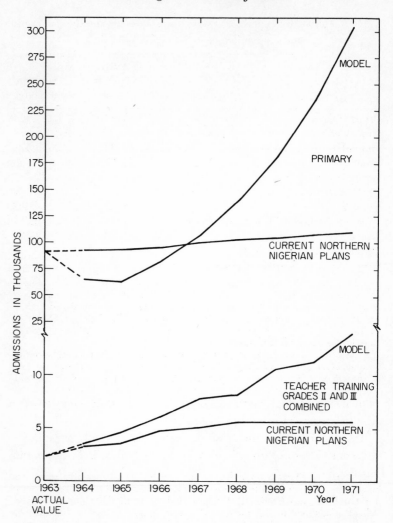

Fig. 16. Primary School and Teacher Training Admissions,
Northern Nigeria, 1964–1971

rate of growth of primary education over the last seven years of the planning period reflects the high ratio of net benefits to both social cost per student and inputs of teachers in the primary school activity. More explicitly, one can say that the strong claim on resources exerted by primary education is due in large measure to the low opportunity cost of its major inputs; the opportunity cost of student time (a major input for other activities) is zero, and the opportunity cost of Grade II and Grade III teachers in the economy is minute compared to the opportunity cost of university graduates, who form the bulk of teaching staffs at postprimary institutions.

The initial decline in primary school admissions indicated in Figure 16 is explained largely by the planned upgrading of the primary school teaching staffs (see Figure 15) and the rather complicated interrelations between primary schools and teacher training. We have found that there are a number of activities within the educational system which are particularly closely intertwined and that the reciprocal, and even multilateral, trading of continuing students and teachers often results in a somewhat unexpected pattern of optimal educational growth. The connection between primary education and the two major types of primary school teacher training (Grades II and III) is a good example of this problem (see Figure 17). Grade III teachers have three years of postprimary education and are the lowest category of trained teachers in the primary schools. Grade II teachers have a total of five years of postprimary training. Primary school graduates are an input into Grade III teacher-training courses (see Table 4). The outputs of the Grade III course are delivered back to the primary school teaching staff or to the Grade II training course for further training. Those who successfully complete the Grade II course serve as teachers in the primary schools or as student inputs into the higher teacher-training institutions. Thus, while it is not exactly true

113

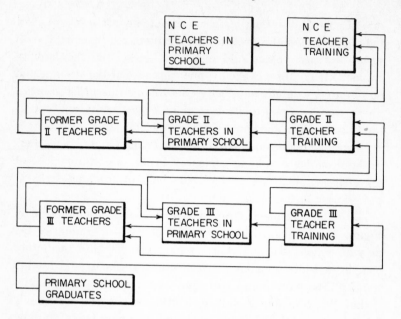

Fig. 17. Recruitment and Training of Primary School Teachers
in Northern Nigeria

that everything depends on everything else (this particular whirl-pool of interdependence appears to be relatively self-contained), each activity level does relate to a number of others, often in a rather complicated way.

Recall that as part of the program of quality improvement in primary school teaching the relatively well-trained Grade II teachers are being substituted for Grade III teachers and the untrained. The upward movement of the Grade II teacher input coefficient over time requires that in addition to training teachers to accommodate the increment in total enrollments, the Grade II teacher-training course must produce a sufficient number to effect an increase in the Grade II teacher coefficient, not only for the increment in enrollments, but for the entire stock of primary students currently in the process of being educated.

The educational system can choose among four alternative methods of acquiring the necessary Grade II teachers: 1) it can admit primary school graduates into the three-year Grade III course and admit those who successfully complete the course into the Grade II course; 2) it can withdraw Grade III teachers from teaching in primary schools and admit them to the Grade II course; 3) it can recruit former Grade III teachers from the nonteaching labor force and admit them to the Grade II course; or 4) it can recruit former Grade II teachers from the nonteaching labor force.

All four methods are used. However, it is the withdrawal of Grade III teachers from the primary schools for further training which is largely responsible for the early decline in primary school admissions. The process is analogous to a temporary cutback in production to allow for retooling of the existing capital stock, followed by a rapid expansion with a new technology. Were the system restricted to channeling school graduates through the usual Grade III and Grade II sequence, a total of five years would elapse before an increased volume of Grade II output could be made available to the primary schools. In this case, either admissions would have to be significantly reduced or the upgrading of the primary school teaching staff would have to be postponed, or both. A number of runs in which the recruitment of former teachers from the nonteaching labor force was not allowed resulted in a much more pronounced and more prolonged reduction in primary school admissions. On the other hand, a run incorporating no temporal change in the teacher-student ratios (no upgrading of the primary school staffs) resulted in a monotonically increasing admissions level for primary education.

In addition to the dramatic increase in primary school enrollments, a second interesting aspect of the solution is that secondary education and Form VI admit the constrained minimum number of students for all but one year. This is not surprising

115

in view of the relatively small net benefits of secondary education and the significant net costs of Form VI. The solution of the model suggests that attention might be given to the following problems: the high failure rates at these two institutions; the possibility that present technologies are unnecessarily intensive in the use of graduate teachers; the small size of the institutions and the resulting failure to take advantage of substantial potential economies of scale in the production of secondary education; and the possibility that the academic orientation of the curriculum in these two activities is related to the low earnings-streams of the graduates. Secondary education in Northern Nigeria is designed not as a terminal course, but primarily as a preparation for higher education.

A third characteristic of the solution is that the scarcity of Form VI graduates necessitates a very small admission to university education (Table 8). The constraint on the use of Form VI graduates is active in all but two years. (The current Northern Nigerian plans appear to be seriously inconsistent, as the planned cumulative admissions to higher education considerably exceed the planned cumulative admissions to Form VI.) This result suggests that university preparation in the Sixth Forms prevents the system from taking advantage of the significant net benefits associated with university education. The fact that all university admissions are to domestic rather than to foreign institutions may appear somewhat surprising in view of the fact that the average cost of sending students abroad is considerably less than the average cost per student in Nigerian universities. Recall, however, that because of the underutilization of facilities (both staff and buildings), the marginal cost is far below the average.

Fourth, the technical training schools admit no students for the entire eight years. Although the present value of the net benefits of the activity is positive, it is not sufficiently great to divert additional resources from other more profitable schooling activities. This result is somewhat surprising in view of the wide-spread belief that technical education should expand as rapidly as possible. (The expansion of technical education is one of the three priority items in the National Development Plan.) It should be made clear that the solution does not suggest that technical education is unnecessary in Northern Nigeria, but rather that, given the present production processes and composition of output, the benefits are not high enough to justify the costs. The cost of operating the present technical training schools is extraordinarily high: capital costs per student place are over twice those at the most expensive nontechnical institutions at the secondary education level; and total social costs per student per year (including foregone earnings) are 1.8 times as high.

Moreover, the demand for technical graduates in Northern Nigeria is very limited. In 1962 (in establishments of ten or more workers), the number of persons employed in mining and quarrying, manufacturing, construction, electricity and water supply, commerce and transport, and communication was less than 100,000, or less than 1 percent of the total labor force.[32] Thus, the demand for the highly trained technicians now being produced is limited to a few government ministries and a handful of industries. A survey of recent graduates of Nigerian technical training schools indicated that a large number are presently holding jobs requiring skills far below those developed in the course of their education.[33] As a consequence of their "overtraining," many of the students graduating from the technical training schools can expect to be employed at jobs in which their marginal productivity is far lower than the minimum necessary to justify the substantial costs of their education.

[32] See Ministry of Economic Planning, *Statistical Yearbook, 1964* (Kaduna: Government Printer, 1964).

[33] Based on records maintained by the Ministry of Education.

The following alterations should be considered: the conversion of the craft school course to a terminal course for a substantial number of students; the possibility of a significant reduction in the costs of the technical training schools; [34] and greater reliance on the in-service training programs run by private industry and the public corporations. (A preliminary survey of two private industry training programs indicated that their benefit cost ratio was considerably higher than that of the government technical training schools.) Were the latter approach adopted, the formal educational system could concentrate on providing general education designed to raise the level of trainability of students rather than on training designed to equip students with specific occupational skills.

The present solution appears to be dominated by the requirements of a rapidly growing primary education system. Resources are devoted principally to those activities which contribute directly or indirectly to the expansion of primary school admissions. It would be interesting to know what the optimal admission levels at postprimary institutions would be if the existing plan with respect to primary education were carried out. For this purpose we have constrained primary school admissions to the levels specified in recent planning documents [35] and have allowed the other activities to attain optimal values given the constraint. The cumulative admissions levels appear in Table 9. This constrained solution generates a net contribution of schooling to the present value of future national income which is 23 percent lower than the above optimal solution. The economic cost of a non-optimal pattern of growth for primary education is apparently considerable.

[34] Expansion of the existing schools rather than the present policy of proliferation of schools is one means to a substantial cost reduction.

[35] See Archer, *Educational Development in Nigeria 1961–70, A Report on the Phasing and Cost of Educational Development on the Basis of the Ashby Commission's Report.*

118

Table 9. Cumulative admissions to postprimary institutions with primary
school admissions from Northern Nigerian plan, 1964–1971

Activity	Current Nigerian Plans	Optimal postprimary admissions with primary school admissions at planned levels
Craft school	a	0
Grade III teacher training	22,800	36,686
Secondary school	51,900	28,971
Grade II teacher training	17,230	23,609
Technical training school	a	0
Form VI	2,560	8,700
Northern Secondary Teachers College	1,335	2,316
University	3,500	3,964
Foreign university	1,000	0

[a] See note b to Table 8.

THE CHOICE OF EDUCATIONAL TECHNIQUES

Many of the policy decisions facing planners in the field of
education concern changes in educational technologies. In this
section we will explore the economic implications of a number
of technological changes in primary education.

The Ministry of Education in Northern Nigeria has recently
given consideration to a proposal which would reduce the number of years in the primary school course. The shorter course
proposed would provide the same number of classroom hours
presently offered in the seven-year course. This is possible because of the relatively short school year in operation under the
present system. The optimality of a similar proposal has been
considered with the model. Primary school activities of five years'

119

duration have been introduced. The *annual* costs are somewhat higher (to allow for the opportunity cost of withdrawing the teaching staff from possible vacation-time employment), but, given the reduction of the course from seven to five years, the total discounted cost is not increased. The teacher-student ratios are unchanged, except that the elimination of the sixth and seventh years obviously releases a significant portion of the teaching staff. Once the system is in operation, overall teacher requirements are reduced to five sevenths of the previous level.[36] In addition, the availability of the primary school output two years earlier increases the present value of the benefits-stream.

The effect of the introduction of the new five-year primary school course can be briefly outlined. The net benefits in the optimal solution are more than 5.8 percent higher than the benefits in the solution based on the present seven-year course. The increase in total net benefits can be explained by the reduction in overall teacher requirements, which, among other things, facilitates the "retooling" process; and by the increase in the present value of net benefits per student due to the shortened period of production.

A number of other runs have tested the implications of the following types of structural or technological change in the production of education: an increase in the university course from three to four years, accompanied by the elimination of the present Sixth Form, the two-year university preparatory course which has constituted a serious bottleneck for university expansion; changes in the failure rates in various teacher-training activities; a less rapid quality improvement in the teaching staffs in primary

---

[36] If one took account of the effect of wastage on the teacher-student ratios, the reduction in overall requirements would be somewhat less. It should be pointed out that the impact of the change is not felt in the model until the sixth year of the plan, because it is assumed that primary school students already in school at the beginning of the plan will remain for the usual seven years.

schools; and various changes in the productive techniques at the primary school level. In each of these cases, a significant increase in net benefits was made possible.

A particularly interesting experiment in productive techniques was the introduction of satellite-broadcast educational television. This experiment was performed in collaboration with Dean Jamison, whose work on the economics of satellite broadcasting provides the basic data for the introduction of television in Northern Nigeria.[37] The hypothetical nature of this exercise should be stressed, in part because the prospect of relying on a technology monopolized by a handful of great powers presents a serious challenge to the sovereignty of any smaller nation using the technique. The resulting political difficulties could be insurmountable.

Despite the fact that it was very conservatively assumed that use of the new technology would bring no reduction in costs, the optimal solution, using the new technology, was characterized by an increase in both primary school enrollments and total benefits. The increase in net benefits despite the absence of any reduction in unit costs is explained by the fact that the introduction of the satellite breaks the teacher bottleneck which, in other solutions, occurs early in the planning period. Stated somewhat differently, if primary school inputs are valued at their shadow prices rather than at their market prices, the satellite effects a considerable reduction in unit costs; teachers are considerably undervalued on the market, particularly in the early years. Breaking the bottleneck allows the primary school system to begin growing at its maximal rate one year earlier and results in a considerable gain in cumulative admissions.

[37] Dean Jamison, "The Optimal Utilization of Communication Satellites for Educational Purposes," American Institute of Aeronautics and Astronautics Paper No. 68–421, April 1968, and "The Economics of Programming for Instructional Broadcast Satellites," AIAA Paper No. 67–787, October 1967.

OPTIMAL TOTAL RESOURCE USE BY EDUCATION

We turn now to the question of total resource use by the educational system. We have two related types of measures of the optimality of the division of resources between education and the rest of the economy: the amount of additional resources recruited into the educational system in the optimal solution, and the shadow prices of resources.

The activities which recruit new factors (for example, former teachers) will be run at positive levels whenever the indirect effect of an additional unit of resource on the discounted value of future GNP is greater than the estimate of the resource's unit cost.[38]

In all solutions of the model, it has been optimal to augment the existing factor supplies with recruits both from the Nigerian labor force outside education and from abroad. Thus, for example, the high level of recruitment of Grade III teachers reflects the fact that the marginal productivity of these personnel (in terms of discounted future national income) when used in the production of primary education is considerably higher than the marginal productivity of the same people when employed in the rest of the economy. The solutions suggest that an increase in primary school teachers' salaries as part of a recruitment drive would be economically profitable. The high level of importation of foreign teachers indicates that during most years of the planning period the value of the marginal product of these teach-

[38] Where z is a row vector of the objective function coefficients, B the basis of included activities, a_k the vector representing the recruiting activity, and c_k the estimated opportunity cost of recruitment, the simplex criterion insures that the recruiting activity will be run at positive levels whenever:
$$c_k < zB^{-1}a_k.$$
The term on the right-hand side of the inequality is the direct and indirect effect of the availability of an additional unit of the resource on the objective function.

ers within the educational system exceeded the rather substantial importation costs.

The shadow prices of each resource provide some indication of the optimal total resource use by the educational system. If the shadow price of the resource within the educational system, measuring the direct and indirect contribution of a unit of the resource to discounted future GNP, exceeds the marginal productivity of the resource in its next best use, then we can conclude that the allocation of more of the resources in question to the educational system would increase the present value of future national income.

Total resource use in the model is measured in money terms and is referred to as total social expenditure on education. This quantity includes the direct social costs of education together with the opportunity costs of students' time incurred during the process of education. In all solutions of the model, the shadow price referring to total social expenditure on education is high relative to any plausible estimate of the marginal productivity of resources in alternative uses. At first glance, one would conclude that a major increase in the availability of resources for the educational system is called for. However, the skeptic and the planner may wish to investigate how the shadow price is affected by changes in the availability of resources to the system.

Parametric programming has been used to estimate the marginal productivity function for expenditures on education. The element in the constraint vector referring to the maximum total expenditure has been first set at a low level and then increased. For higher levels of expenditure, the original solution will no longer be optimal. At the point where each change in the optimal basis occurs, an entire new optimal solution—including total benefits, shadow prices, and optimal activity levels—has been recorded. This technique allows us to trace out both the marginal productivity function for expenditure on education and

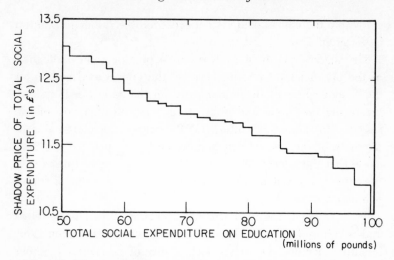

Fig. 18. The Productivity of Resources in Northern Nigerian
Education, Expressed as a Function of Total Social
Expenditure on Education

Notes: Present value of total social expenditure is based on a 5 percent
discount rate. Current planned expenditures is in the neighborhood of £ 80
million.

a function relating the total benefits to total expenditure. The
two functions appear in Figures 18 and 19. The shadow prices
appearing in the step function in Figure 18 are clearly the slopes
of the minute line segments which make up the total benefits
function in Figure 19.[39] The range of variation in the total social
expenditure on education presented here is centered on £80
million, which is about what present government plans imply.
Variations beyond the range presented in the figures are thought
to be of dubious value because the linearity of the relationships
in the model is open to serious question when very major changes
in allocation are being considered.

[39] Although difficult to detect visually, the function in Figure 19 are
concave from below; the implied diminishing marginal productivity is
clearly shown in the negative inclination of the step function in Figure 18.

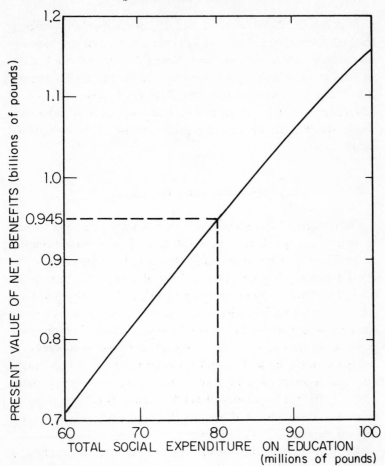

Fig. 19. Present Value of Net Benefits of Education as a Function of Total Social Expenditure on Education, Northern Nigeria

Note: Present values of net benefits and total social expenditures are based on a 5 percent discount rate.

Two aspects of Figures 18 and 19 are particularly striking: the high level of the shadow prices over a wide range of expenditure on education, and the very favorable ratio of net benefits to total costs. These results seem to confirm the earlier impression that a revision of the present division of resources between education and the rest of the economy in favor of education would significantly increase the present value of future national income.

IMPORTING EDUCATED LABOR

The number of foreigners involved in teaching a nation's youth is naturally a question of political as well as economic importance. The replacement of foreign teachers by indigenous teachers is a major policy goal in a number of countries; others place explicit or implicit limits on the proportion of teaching positions which may be held by aliens. Yet foreigners are often a crucial element in expanding the available supply of teachers and are particularly important as a means of breaking bottlenecks in teacher training itself. The optimal importation of foreign teachers thus depends on a trade-off between income (and perhaps other) gains made possible through a more rapid expansion in educational facilities and welfare losses occasioned by an increased dependence on foreigners.

We may expect the social welfare function to contain a negative term relating to the number of imported teachers in the school system. We may write:

$$(10) \quad W = W\,(Y, F, \ldots) \qquad \begin{aligned} &\left(\frac{\partial W}{\partial Y}\right) > 0 \\[2mm] &\left(\frac{\partial W}{\partial F}\right)_{Y \text{ constant}} < 0 \end{aligned}$$

where $W =$ the social welfare function;

$F =$ the total number of teachers imported; and

$Y =$ the present value of future national income.

In view of the fact that over some ranges of importation foreign teachers contribute to the expansion of educational output and hence of future national income, we can further write:

(11) $Y = g(F)$ (all other inputs constant)

and, therefore,

(12) $W = W[g(F), F, \ldots]$.

First-order conditions for the maximum W require that

$$\frac{-\partial W/\partial F}{\partial W/\partial Y} = \frac{\partial Y}{\partial F}$$

or that the marginal rate of substitution in the social welfare function between income and foreigners must equal the marginal product of foreigners or the marginal rate of transformation of foreigners into income.[40]

We can estimate this last relation by using the parametric programming technique described in the previous section. The term $\partial Y/\partial F$ is the shadow price of foreign teachers in the model, or the slope of the function appearing in Figure 20. The shape of the function and the limited range of variation of F between the point of redundancy and the point at which no feasible solution exists suggest that, given the present structure of the system, the productivity of foreigners is high at present levels of use (the shadow price is well above any conceivable cost of

---

[40] For simplicity of presentation, we have here ignored the term $\dfrac{\partial W}{\partial E}\dfrac{\partial E}{\partial F}$ which would take account of the fact that increased importation of foreigners allows an expansion of enrollment (E) which may be valued directly in the social welfare function, apart from the associated income gains.

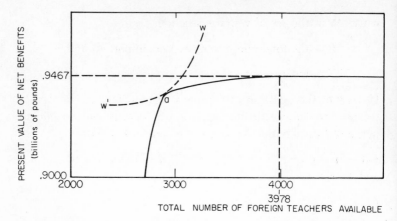

Fig. 20. Present Value of Net Benefits of Education as a Function of the Total Number of Foreign Teachers Available, Northern Nigeria

Note: The shadow price falls to zero when 3,978 foreign teachers are available. In the normal optimal solution, 3,762 were imported. Because of the annual constraints on the maximum number of foreign teachers available, the total benefits generated in the normal optimal solution (Figure 19) are slightly below the analogous level in Figure 20.

importing), though any major increase in importation would quickly depress their marginal product to zero. Nonetheless, the high shadow price of foreigners over the relevant range is suggestive of a rather major opportunity cost of pursuing nationalistic educational policies. The dotted line WW′ in that figure represents a hypothetical nationalistic social-welfare function which yields an optimum at point a. Figure 21, showing the shadow prices of both foreign teachers and total social expenditure, suggests that foreign teachers and domestic resources are complementary in the production of Nigerian education.[41]

[41] More specifically:

$$\frac{\partial^2 Z}{\partial C \partial F} > 0$$

when C $\doteq$ total social expenditure on education.

128

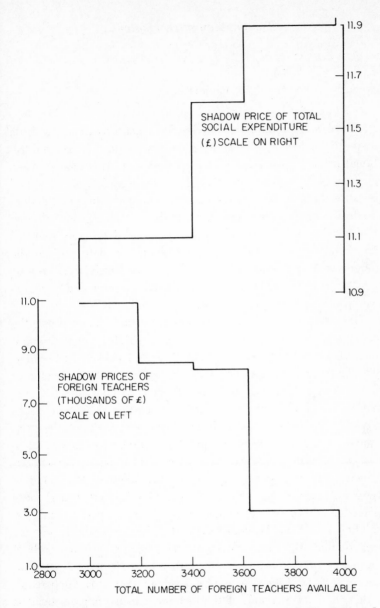

Fig. 21. Shadow Prices of Foreign Teachers and Total Social
Expenditure as a Function of Total Foreign Teachers
Available, Northern Nigeria

Conclusions

The planning model presented here was constructed as a guide to public policy in education. Its main purpose is to establish broad priorities for educational development. This has not been an easy task, because much of the data is subject to error and because the assumptions required to render the problem mathematically manageable have had to be something less than a faithful replica of the real world. Analysis of the sensitivity of the solution to the presence of error in the data and to the unreality in the assumptions allows us to identify those results which are invariant to a plausible degree of error and in which we may, therefore, place considerable confidence.

Three types of sensitivity analysis were undertaken. First, the objective function was re-estimated using a 10 percent discount rate, and new solutions computed. Second, I calculated the margin (both positive and negative) by which each parameter of the objective function could be in error without affecting the pattern of enrollments in the optimal solution. The same technique was used on the right-hand-side constants in the constraint equations. These computations provide estimates of a margin of error for each parameter. Third, parameters about which there was particular doubt were allowed to assume a range of alternative values. Solutions computed using these plausible alternative estimates were then compared with the solution based on the actual estimates. For example, it was assumed that the unemployment rate among primary school graduates would be 20 percent, rather than 10 percent, over an entire lifetime. Likewise, it was assumed that only 60 percent, rather than 100 percent, of the increment in earnings associated with additional schooling could be attributed to the effects of education.[42]

In light of this sensitivity analysis, let us review the major inferences for educational policy which can be drawn from this model.

First, rapid expansion of primary education is a top priority item, using any plausible estimates.

Second, given the present costs, no reasonable future increase in the demand for technicians would be sufficient to provide an economic rationale for the expansion of secondary technical education. The model clearly indicates the desirability of investigating alternative methods of producing the needed technical skills.

Third, given the bottlenecks in the teacher supply, there are very high returns to be expected from the additional recruitment of both primary school and other teachers, even at considerably higher salaries. Similarly, high returns are associated with quality improvements in the teacher-training colleges designed to lower the failure rates at these institutions.

Fourth, despite the obvious limitations of the estimates which comprise the objective function, I am confident in stating that a diversion of additional resources to the education sector would result in an increase in the present value of future national income. This policy prescription is not affected either by the use of a higher discount rate or by the attribution of a smaller fraction of the earnings differences to the unique effects of schooling. For example, assuming that 60 percent of the earnings differences among workers classified by educational level are attributable to differences in schooling, the net benefits are still about seven

---

[42] Much of the sensitivity analysis was performed on a slightly different, earlier version of the model. I do not believe that any of the recent changes in the model have vitiated any of the general conclusions.

times as large as total social expenditures. The shadow price of social expenditure is £6.6.

Fifth, while neither higher nor general secondary education exerts any major claim on resources at existing levels of total expenditure on education, at more nearly optimal levels of total resource use the universities (both at home and abroad) show substantial increases in enrollments. On the other hand, given the present curriculum and cost structure, the economic justification of the secondary educational system is apparently confined to the production of students for admission to higher education.

Sixth, the high returns on a variety of technical changes in the production of education suggest that additional effort and research should be devoted to the development and adaptation of new pedagogical techniques, new equipment, and structural changes in the schooling system.

It may seem surprising, or even incredible, that a relatively simple model can yield a series of important policy prescriptions which are not easily reversed by any plausible degree of error in the data or the assumptions. Experience in market economies in the analysis of more conventional economic policy problems, such as taxation and tariffs, suggests that in the absence of reasonably good data, little can be said; and, even with the best of information, estimates of the quantitative gains to be expected from the adoption of economically optimal policies tend to be small.[43]

The possibility of unambiguous prescriptions and the large expected gains through a more efficient resource allocation in education may be explained in part by the nature of educational decision-making. Because of the absence of any explicit eco-

[43] For a survey, see Harvey Leibenstein, "Allocative Efficiency vs. 'X-Efficiency'," *American Economic Review*, vol. 56, no. 3 (June 1966), pp. 392–415.

nomically oriented optimizing behavior on the part of school administrators and because of the difficulty in viewing the system as one of rather general interaction, the existing resource allocation in most education systems is far more inefficient (in purely economic terms) than the resource allocation in the more market-oriented sectors, where the necessity to survive forces some degree of optimizing behavior on the decision-makers and where the market takes account of at least some of the interactions between participants. Given this situation, a simple economic analysis of the educational sector which takes account of the general equilibrium nature of the sector's internal intertemporal relations can be expected to yield policy prescriptions which result in rather substantial gains in the economic efficiency of the system.

V · Alternative Approaches
to Educational Planning:
An Empirical Comparison

Economists and educators have a wide range of choice in the selection of a method for educational planning.[1] The following comparison is based on recent empirical applications of four different planning methods to the Greek educational system. I will begin with two variations on the manpower requirements approach, then move on to the rate-of-return method, and conclude with the intertemporal linear programming model developed in the previous chapter. A brief introduction to the Greek economy and educational system will be helpful in interpreting the models.

EDUCATION IN THE GREEK ECONOMY

Compared to most poor countries, and particularly to our previous case study, Northern Nigeria, education in Greece is both abundant and cheap. These two characteristics will have a strong bearing on the planning of optimal resource allocations over the next decade or so.

The structure of the Greek educational system is depicted in Table 10 as a matrix of intra-educational flows of continuing

[1] For a general survey of alternative planning techniques in the field of education, see Mark Blaug, "Alternative Approaches to Educational Planning," *Economic Journal,* June 1967, pp. 262–287.

Table 10. The structure of the Greek educational system [a]

Producing sectors	Usual age of entry (years)	Duration of course (years)	Using sectors								Labor market
			1	2	3	4	5	6	7	8	
1. Primary school	6	6	—	S	—	S	—	—	—	—	L
2. Gymnasium (first cycle, secondary)	12	3	—	—	S	—	—	—	—	—	L
3. Lyceum (second cycle, secondary)	15	3	—	—	—	—	—	S	—	S	L
4. Technical schools (lower)	12	3	—	—	—	—	S	—	—	—	L
5. Technical schools (middle)	15	3	—	—	—	—	—	—	S	—	L
6. Pedagogical academy	18+	3	T	—	—	—	—	—	—	—	—
7. School for Assistant Engineers	18+	4	—	—	—	T	T	—	—	—	L
8. University											
Arts, humanities	18+	4	—	T	T	—	—	T	—	T	L
Mathematics, physics, and related subjects		4	—	T	T	—	—	T	—	T	L
Engineering and related subjects		4	—	T	T	—	—	T	—	T	L

[a] S indicates a flow of students from the indicated row to the indicated column; T indicates a flow of teachers from the indicated row to the indicated column; L in the column "Labor market" indicates that the producing sector delivers labor to the force outside education.

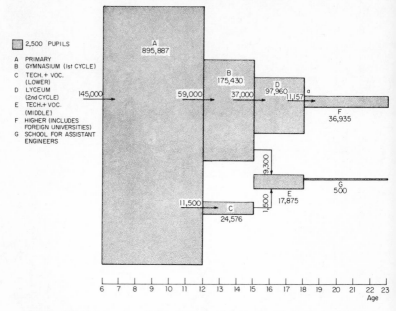

Fig. 22. Structure of the Greek Educational System, 1961

Sources: The Mediterranean Regional Project, *Country Reports, Greece* (OECD: Paris, 1965), p. 178.

[a] Includes students going abroad.

students and teachers. A companion diagram (Figure 22) presents the magnitudes of the stocks and flows of students for the year 1961 in the usual form of an educational pyramid.

Primary education is compulsory from age six through the completion of six years, a requirement to which virtually all children conform. Secondary general education is divided into two cycles, the gymnasium and the lyceum. In 1961 almost half the successful primary school graduates were admitted to the first cycle of the secondary school course—the gymnasium. The retardation and wastage (dropout) rates for both the gymnasium and lyceum are high, as can be seen in Appendix 5.

Table 11. Percentage distribution of teachers in Greek public secondary general schools by field of specialization, 1961

Specialization	Percentage
Theology	10.0
Literature	43.4
Mathematics	15.0
Physics—Chemistry	10.9
Commercial subjects	1.4
Foreign languages	4.0
Home economics	2.5
Music	1.7
Gymnastics	11.1
Total	100.0

Source: The Mediterranean Regional Project, *Country Reports, Greece* (Paris: OECD, 1965), p. 80.

The curriculum in the lyceum (the second cycle of general secondary education) has traditionally been heavily oriented toward the study of the classics and the humanities and is regarded primarily as a preparation for higher education. The subject emphasis in the Greek school system at both the gymnasium and lyceum levels is clearly shown in Table 11, which presents data on the number of teachers by specialization in the period 1961.[2]

Many vocational and technical educational programs are offered at the secondary level. In a number of respects these courses are not an integral part of the formal schooling system. They are generally privately run by part-time staffs for part-time students. Students usually attend night sessions, and staff members are often paid at hourly rates. Moreover, at the present time, the secondary-level vocational courses are dead ends in that those

[2] More recent data for the years 1964–1965 indicate a substantially unchanged distribution.

who successfully complete the course are not expected to continue their education within the formal schooling system. Nonetheless, because of the central role they have played in recent discussions of the economics of Greek education, these vocational programs deserve some consideration.

At least four types of higher education will be distinguished. Successful graduates from the lyceum can enter a pedagogical institute for training, after three years of which they are eligible to become primary school teachers. Alternatively, lyceum graduates may enter a university and study in any of the usual fields, which I have grouped under the headings: humanities and social sciences, mathematics and physical sciences, and engineering and related subjects. The university facilities available in Greece are supplemented for a large number of students by higher education in foreign countries.

The level of schooling in the Greek labor force is roughly similar to that in countries which are at approximately the same level of development; Greece, unlike Nigeria, does not suffer from severe educational shortages. Table 12 shows the stock of

Table 12. Composition of labor force (male) by highest level of education completed (in percent) in selected countries

Country	Year [a]	Income/capita in 1957 dollars (income in 1958)	Not finished primary	Primary	Secondary	Higher
Chile	1960	335	57.7	35.4	5.6	1.3
Colombia	1961	192	92.2	4.0	2.8	1.0
Greece	1961	273	37.0	51.1	8.4	3.5
India	1961	64	89.9	7.3	2.3	0.5
Israel	1957	671	20.3	44.0	27.0	8.7
Italy	1961	428	39.8	52.3	4.8	3.1
Mexico	1960	283	79.9	17.7	1.2	1.1

Source: References cited in Appendix 1.

[a] Year refers to distribution of labor force.

138

labor classified by years of schooling in the Greek labor force compared with the labor stock in other countries. Total school enrollments in Greece constitute a larger fraction of the five to twenty-four age group than do school enrollments in a number of more affluent nations, including West Germany, Italy, and Austria.

By most standards, schooling in Greece is relatively inexpensive. This is true whether we measure the costs in market prices, expressed in some common currency, or whether we measure the resource inputs into education in physical terms. Teacher-pupil ratios are lower than in most European countries, and considerably lower than in Northern Nigeria.[3] Because of the very low resource use per student in Greek education (despite the large number of students enrolled in schools and universities), the percentage of gross national product devoted to education is relatively small compared to that in other countries. (See Table 13.)

For the past few years economic planners and educators have had to grapple with a number of interesting and economically important policy issues. Among these, perhaps the most important are: (1) Is Greece overeducated? Would the productivity of resources currently being devoted to schooling be higher if they were transferred to some more directly productive activity? (2) Is the specialization of students of higher education in the present categories optimal from an economic standpoint? More concretely, should a larger number of students enroll in engineering and scientific courses? (3) What are the economic costs of and returns on university level study abroad? (4) Is there an economic rationale for the rapid expansion of the gymnasia, as was required by the 1964 reform which made schooling com-

[3] However, compared to similar countries, the training of the teaching staff is relatively good: most primary school teachers have at least two years of postsecondary education, and virtually all secondary school teachers possess a university degree.

Table 13. Total educational expenditure as a percentage
of GNP in selected countries

Country	Percentage of GNP spent on education 1957–1958 [a]
U.S.S.R.	7.1
Finland	6.3
Japan	5.7
United States	4.6
United Kingdom	4.2
Egypt	3.7
Burma	3.6
West Germany	3.6
Cuba	3.4
Italy	3.2
France	3.0
Tanzania	3.0
Yugoslavia	2.8
Thailand	2.7
Turkey	2.2
Nigeria	1.9
India	1.7
Greece	1.6
Spain	1.4

Source: Frederick Harbison and Charles A. Myers, *Education, Manpower and Economic Growth: Strategies of Human Resource Development.* Inter-University Study of Labor Problems in Economic Development, Princeton University Industrial Relations Section and M.I.T. (New York: McGraw-Hill Book Co., Inc., 1964), tables 5–8, pp. 45–48.

[a] The figures refer either to the year 1957–58, or to the closest year to that date for which data were available.

pulsory up to age fifteen? [4] (5) Should greater emphasis be placed on vocational rather than general education at the secondary level?

[4] The 1964 reform was legislated under the leadership of George Papandreou, then prime minister. Since the military coup of 1967, the status of the reform has been unclear.

We turn now to the four distinct economic methods designed to provide answers to these or similar questions and to determine the correct allocation of resources in the educational system over the next decade. Throughout the remainder of this chapter, I have adopted the period 1961–1974 as the relevant planning period. This period corresponds roughly to the planning period used by the OECD's Mediterranean Regional Project.

THE MANPOWER REQUIREMENTS APPROACH

The manpower requirements approach to educational planning may be described as an attempt to derive required educational outputs from a set of economic growth projections.[5] Specifically, economic growth forecasts or targets are used to predict the sectoral distribution of output and employment in some future year. The sectoral distribution of employment is converted to an occupational distribution of the total labor force. The distribution of the labor force by level of schooling is computed from the distribution of workers by occupation. The resulting estimates of the "required" numbers of workers classified by education level can then be used in conjunction with data on existing stocks and expected retirement rates to generate a plan of necessary enrollment levels in various types of educational institutions. This general method of educational planning has been widely used. The current educational plans of Nigeria, Zambia, Tanzania,

[5] In the description of the manpower requirements method I will draw heavily on the Mediterranean Regional Project, *Country Reports, Greece* (Paris: OECD, 1965). The manpower requirements method is spelled out in greater detail in Herbert Parnes, *Forecasting Educational Needs for Economic and Social Development,* The Mediterranean Regional Project (Paris: OECD, 1962). For a good critical review of the Mediterranean Regional Project's method, see Robinson Hollister, *A Technical Evaluation of the First Stage of the Mediterranean Regional Project* (Paris: OECD, 1966).

Kenya, West Germany, the U.S.S.R., and a number of other countries are in large part the result of this type of planning.[6]

The Mediterranean Regional Project of the OECD is perhaps the largest single educational planning exercise yet attempted. As part of this project, the governments of six member countries (Turkey, Spain, Yugoslavia, Italy, Greece, and Portugal) undertook to develop long-term educational plans in conjunction with separate teams of planners working under the auspices of the OECD Secretariat. The Greek team of the Mediterranean Regional Project completed its work and published its report early in 1965.

We may briefly review the steps by which the Mediterranean Regional Project Team in Greece arrived at its estimates of the required development of schooling. First, output (gross domestic product at factor cost at 1961 prices) was projected for the period up to 1974.[7] Total output was divided into eight economic sectors. Second, total labor productivity in each sector was estimated, although there is no systematic discussion of how these

[6] Nigeria: see J. N. Archer, *Educational Development in Nigeria, 1961–70: A Report on the Planning and Cost of Educational Development on the Basis of the Ashby Commission's Report* (Lagos: Government Printer, 1961).

Zambia: see Manpower Report: *A Report on Manpower, Education and Training in Zambia* (Lusaka: Government Printer, 1966).

Tanzania: see R. L. Thomas, *Survey of the High Level Manpower Requirements and Resources for the Five-Year Development Plan, 1964/65 to 1968/69* (Dar-es-Salaam: Government Printer, 1965).

Kenya: see Calvin F. Davis, *High Level Manpower Requirements and Resources in Kenya, 1964–70* (Nairobi: Government Press, 1965).

West Germany: see H. P. Widmaier, "A Case Study of Educational Planning: Western Germany," in G. Z. F. Bereday, J. A. Lauwerys, and Mark Blaug (eds.), *Education Planning: The World Year Book of Education* (London: Evans Bros. Ltd., 1967, and New York: Harcourt Brace & World, Inc., 1967), which contains further examples.

U.S.S.R.: see Nicholas DeWitt, *Educational and Professional Employment in the U.S.S.R.* (Washington: National Science Foundation, 1961).

[7] These projections were based on data supplied by the Ministry of Coordination. Further projections beyond 1974 were made by the Mediterranean Regional Project Team.

142

projections were made. The combination of sectoral output levels and estimates of labor productivity by sector allowed the computation of the distribution of the labor force by sector. Third, the total labor force in each sector was broken down into a total of sixty-two occupational classifications. This step was based on a detailed investigation of existing occupational distributions by sector and on educated guesses concerning likely changes in the occupational structure over the planning period. The number of workers in each occupational classification was then summed over all sectors to arrive at the total number of "required" occupations in the terminal year 1974. Fourth, the Mediterranean Regional Project Team next estimated the amount of education required for the performance of each of the sixty-two jobs. For example, it was assumed that 40 percent of the new managers during the period 1961–1974 would have to have an economics or commercial degree. Similarly, it was assumed that 20 percent of the new civil service administrators would be graduates of law faculties, while the remainder would be graduates of the higher school of political science.[8] Fifth, having thus arrived at an estimate of the total labor force of 1974 by "'required" level of schooling, the Team estimated the necessary enrollment levels, using data on the existing stocks in the year 1961 and the expected attrition on the existing stock through death and retirement. Additional adjustments took into account the expected nonparticipation in the labor force of some fraction of those receiving schooling.

Enrollment levels for primary education and general secondary education were planned on the basis of demographic considerations and social demand rather than on the basis of the manpower requirements approach. Thus, the manpower requirements method was strictly applied only to higher and technical educa-

[8] Mediterranean Regional Project, *Country Reports, Greece* (Paris: OECD, 1965), p. 139.

tion. After all the required or desired enrollment levels had been estimated, the demand for new teachers was then computed and added to the totals.[9] The resulting cumulative number of required graduates from higher education appears in Table 14. The basic data on the total enrollment levels and annual flows of students in the terminal year, 1974, are presented in Figure 23 as a terminal year educational pyramid. Although the results will be discussed in greater detail in the concluding section, the broad outlines can be stated here. The most rapid rates of growth and enrollment are for secondary schools, particularly those offering technical courses. Enrollment at the university level is required to shift appreciably toward engineering and the physical sciences.

A Modified Manpower Requirements Approach

A method of educational planning which is similar in spirit, although different in important details, is the method developed by Tinbergen and Correa in 1962.[10] This has provided the analytical framework for educational planning in India and Uganda.[11] The same method, which I shall call the Tinbergen approach,

[9] The addition of a number of teachers to the required level of output at some levels must certainly have produced repercussions at other levels which would have, in a more systematic treatment, required adjustments throughout the system. The team was aware of this difficulty but thought it to be quantitatively insignificant. Mediterranean Regional Project, *Country Reports, Greece,* p. 160.

[10] Hector Correa and Jan Tinbergen, "Quantitative Adaptation of Education to Accelerated Growth," *Kyklos,* 15 (1962), pp. 776–785.

[11] See E. R. Rado and A. R. Jolly, "The Demand for Manpower: An East African Case Study," *Journal of Development Studies,* vol. 1, no. 3 (April 1965). See also T. Burgess, P. R. G. Layard, and Pitamber Pant, *Manpower and Educational Development in India (1961–86)* (London: Oliver and Boyd, 1968). The model has also been applied in Turkey and Spain, for which see Jan Tinbergen and H. C. Bos, *Econometric Models of Education, Some Applications* (Paris: OECD, 1965).

Table 14. Total number of graduates required from higher education by faculty, Greece, 1962–1974, as planned by the Mediterranean Regional Project

Faculty	Total [a]
Engineering and related fields	10,660
Agriculture	2,260
Architecture	1,060
Civil engineering	3,870
Forestry	420
Mechanical/electrical engineering	1,740
Mining engineering	230
Veterinary medicine	460
Mathematics and physical sciences	5,050
Chemistry	2,550
Mathematics	160
Pharmaceutics	1,790
Physics and natural sciences	550
Humanities and social sciences	29,500
Economics and business administration	11,010
Law	10,690
Literature (including foreign languages)	1,700
Political science	5,150
Schools of art, etc.	380
Theology	570

Source: The Mediterranean Regional Project, *Country Reports, Greece* (Paris: OECD, 1965), p. 141.

[a] Including "leakages" of graduates out of the system, i.e., those graduates who will not seek employment in occupations relevant to the Plan, and excluding requirements for teachers.

was applied to Greek data in the period 1964–65 by Gareth Williams.[12] Although actual solutions to the model were computed, the purpose of the exercise was not to define an educational

[12] Gareth Williams, "Planning Models for the Calculation of Educational Requirements for Economic Development, Greece," in Tinbergen and Bos, *Econometric Models of Education,* pp. 77–93.

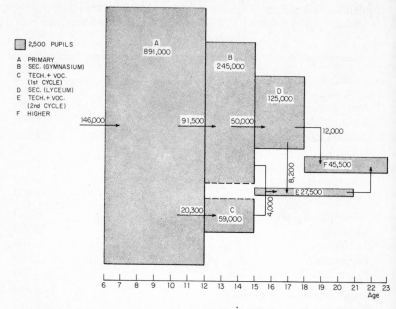

Fig. 23. Structure of the Greek Educational System, 1974, as Planned by the Mediterranean Regional Project

Source: The Mediterranean Regional Project, *Country Reports, Greece* (Paris: OECD, 1965), p. 179.

plan, but to explore the empirical and other characteristics of the method.

This approach proceeds at a much higher level of aggregation than the manpower requirements method does. Considerable simplicity is achieved by circumventing the relation of output to occupational distribution and by using instead an estimated direct relationship between aggregate output and the educational level of the labor force. Moreover, in contrast to the manpower requirements approach as used by the Mediterranean Regional Project, the Tinbergen method takes explicit account of the internal productive relations of the educational system. The set of equations describing the input-output relations of the educational system along with equations representing the demand for educated labor in the economy are used to derive a set of required enrollments from an exogenously given rate of economic growth.[13]

The model distinguishes two levels of education—secondary and higher; primary education is assumed to be no bottleneck for the required expansion of secondary education and for production increases in the economy. The time unit chosen was six years, this being the supposed training period for both secondary and higher education.

The following symbols are used, leaving out the time superscript t:

v = the total volume of production (income) of the country;

N^2 = the labor force with a secondary education;

N^3 = the labor force with a third-level education;

m^2 = those who have entered the labor force, N^2, within the previous six years;

m^3 = those who have entered the labor force, N^3, within the previous six years;

n^2 = the number of students in secondary education;

n^3 = the number of students in third-level education;

ν^2, ν^3 = the constants of proportionality for the development of second- and third-level education (respectively) with national production, the inverse of the average productivity of each type of labor;

λ_2, λ_3 = the proportions of the labor force of educational levels two and three who drop out during the six-year period;

a^2, a^3 = the labor force participation rate of recent graduates of educational levels two and three, respectively;

δ^2, δ^3 = the number of graduates of second- and third-level edu-

---

[13] The following description closely follows Tinbergen and Bos, *Econometric Models of Education,* p. 11, and the modifications proposed by Williams on p. 83 of the same volume.

cation who graduate in a six-year period expressed as a proportion of students of the same level at the end of the previous period $(t-1)$;

γ^3 = the number of secondary school graduates who have entered higher education considered as a proportion of the number of students in higher education at the end of the period;

σ^3 = the number of university students who drop out in a six-year period expressed as a proportion of the university population at the end of the previous period;

π^2, π^3 = teacher/student ratios at levels two and three, respectively.

The following relationships are assumed to hold between these variables:

(1) $N_t^2 = \nu^2 v_t$

(2) $N_t^2 = (1 - \lambda^2) \, N_{t-1}^2 + m_t^2$

(3) $m_t^2 = a^2 \left(\delta^2 n_{t-1}^2 - \gamma^3 n_t^3 + \sigma^3 n_{t-1}^3 \right)$

(4) $m_t^3 = a^3 \delta^3 n_{t-1}^3$

(5) $N_t^3 = (1 - \lambda^3) \, N_{t-1}^3 + m_t^3$

(6) $N_t^3 = \nu^3 v_t + \pi^2 n_t^2 + \pi^3 n_t^3$

These equations express the following relationships:

Equation (1): The labor force with a secondary education is used for production only and must develop proportionally with the volume of national production;

Equations (2) and (5): The labor force consists of those already in it one time unit earlier and those who have joined it during the previous six years. It is assumed that a proportion, λ^2 and λ^3, respectively, of those already in the labor force, one time unit earlier, has dropped out because of death or retirement;

Equation (3): The number of newcomers to the labor force with a secondary education is equal to the number of students, one time unit earlier, minus the number of students now in third-level education, adjusted for the appropriate participation and wastage rates;

Equation (4): The number of newcomers to the labor force with a third-level education is equal to the number of third-level students, one time unit earlier, adjusted for labor force participation;

Equation (6): The labor force with a third-level education consists of those employed in production, assumed to be proportional in numbers to the volume of production, and of those teaching at both levels of education and assumed to be proportional to the respective student numbers.

In the application of this model to Greece, Williams used the parameter values as indicated in Table 15. The pattern of re-

Table 15. Tinbergen approach: coefficients for Greece
(values in base period)

Active labor force	Total population
$\nu^3 = 0.0103$	$\nu^{3'} = 0.008$
$\nu^2 = 0.1570$	$\nu^{2'} = 0.093$
$\pi^3 = 0.028$	$\alpha^2 = 0.59$
$\pi^2 = 0.030$	$\gamma^3 = 1.3$
$\lambda^3 = 0.05$	$\delta^3 = 1.4$
$\lambda^2 = 0.04$	$\sigma^3 = 0.3$
$\alpha^3 = 0.85$	$\delta^2 = 0.8$

Source: Jan Tinbergen and H. C. Bos, *Econometric Models of Education, Some Applications* (Paris: OECD, 1965), p. 84.

Table 16. Tinbergen approach: actual values of the manpower and educational variables in the base period, required values for a balanced equilibrium growth of 6 percent per annum (basic model), and forecasts of size of population aged 12–17, Greece

Variables [a]	Actual values	Equilibrium values			
		1961	1967	1973	1980
N^2	289.3	289.3	410.8	583.3	823.3
N^3	74.3	84.1	119.4	169.5	240.7
n^2	273.4	509.9	724.1	1,028.2	1,460.0
n^3	37.1	35.7	50.7	72.0	102.2
m^2	—	95.8	136.0	193.1	274.2
m^3	—	27.7	39.3	55.8	79.2
Population aged 12–17	763.6	763.6	840.6	895.3	914.0

Source: Jan Tinbergen and H. C. Bos, *Econometric Models of Education, Some Applications* (Paris: OECD, 1965), p. 86.

[a] See text for explanation of variables.

quired educational development generated in this model, using the Greek government's target rate of growth of gross domestic product (6 percent per annum), is indicated in Table 16. The most extraordinary characteristic of this particular solution is the fact that the required level of enrollment in secondary education in the base year is nearly twice the actual value and, moreover, that the secondary-level education enrollment is required to rise so rapidly that, twelve years from the base period ($t = 2$), the required enrollment of second-level students exceeds the population in the appropriate age group.

One might conclude that a long-run rate of growth of 6 percent is simply unattainable. However, Williams rejects this inference and instead suggests that the anomalous solution may in fact result from a misspecification of the basic equations describing the requirements for educated labor in the model, namely, equations (1) and (6). On the basis of a cross-section regression analysis of twenty-three countries carried out by the Netherlands Economic Institute, the alternative relationship (6a) is suggested.[14]

$$(6a) \quad N_t^3 = .01062 \, V_t^{1.22} \left(\frac{V_t}{P_t} \right)^{-0.28} + \pi^2 n_t^2 + \pi^3 n_t^3$$

where

a_t = population in period t.

The alternative equation for (1) is:

$$(1a) \quad N_t^2 = 0.0531 \, V_t^{1.22} \left(\frac{V_t}{P_t} \right)^{-0.28}$$

The economy's requirements for secondary-level education in this equation are identical to (6a) except for the constant. Williams selected this equation because "in general it appears that countries have about five times as many second-level people in the labor force as third level."[15]

The introduction of these new relationships allows for increases in the productivity of second- and third-level labor. The resulting modification in the required enrollment values is relatively minor. Moreover, the use of the cross-section estimates, equations (1a)

[14] Equations (6a) and (1a) below are similar, but not identical, to those used in my Chapter III, based on the work reported in The Division of Balanced International Growth in the Netherlands Economic Institute, "Financial Aspects of Education in Developing Areas: Some Quantitative Estimates," in Lucille Reifman (ed.), *Financing of Education for Economic Growth* (Paris: OECD, 1966), pp. 59–72. I am unable to explain the minor discrepancies between Williams' equations and those reported by the Netherlands Economic Institute.

[15] Tinbergen and Bos, *Econometric Models of Education,* p. 86. Data presented in Williams' article and elsewhere in the cited volume suggest that there is no consistent relationship between the number of second- and third-level people. See Williams, "Planning Models for the Calculation of Educational Requirements for Economic Development, Greece," especially p. 97.

and (6a), suggests the following relationship between the required and actual stock of labor in 1961.[16]

	Actual	Required
N^3 (higher)	64.2	32.3
N^2 (secondary)	289.3	161.6

There is nothing inconsistent about this finding. It may be, for example, that Greece is overeducated, or that educated labor is being used inefficiently, or that, because of the content of the curriculum or because of low quality, educated labor in Greece is not as productive as it is in other countries. But as a basis for the planning of school enrollments, the results present some difficulties, as one does not know if the targets should be established on the basis of actual stocks in the base year and required rates of growth or on the basis of required levels of stocks of educated labor in all time periods.

In a further exercise, Williams generates solutions using a value of v^2 (the inverse of average productivity of N^2), which is made to decline by 20 percent during each six-year period. This procedure is quite arbitrary, and, while the resulting solutions are at least feasible, their usefulness to planners must be seriously questioned.[17]

The Rate-of-return Approach

This third approach to educational planning must be set apart from the manpower requirements approach and the Tinbergen method. Unlike the first two, the rate-of-return method is characterized by an explicit attempt to measure both the economic

[16] The figures exclude teachers.

[17] Williams suggests that v^2 fell at approximately this rate over the course of the 1950's, as did v^3. To change only one parameter seems peculiar. Williams, "Planning Models for the Calculation of Educational Requirements," pp. 86–92.

benefits and the costs of schooling. Rather than attempt to estimate the level of schooling required by a particular pattern of economic growth, practitioners of the rate-of-return approach seek to estimate the social profitability of particular types of schooling expenditures. Rates of return on resources devoted to schooling have been estimated for a large number of countries, although in many cases the estimates were conceived of as academic exercises somewhat removed from the day-to-day process of planning educational enrollment and resource allocation.[18] Harvey Leibenstein recently estimated rates of return on secondary and higher education in Greece.[19] We turn now to a brief survey of his methods, data, and results.

Two basic sets of data are needed to compute the rate of return on additional years of schooling: a series of earnings data classified by level of schooling and age of worker, and data on the direct costs of schooling. The earnings data for Leibenstein's study come largely from a sample survey of workers in com-

[18] A. C. Harberger, "Investment in Men vs. Investment in Machines: The Case of India," in C. A. Anderson and M. J. Bowman (eds.), *Education and Economic Development* (London: Frank Cass Co., 1965), pp. 11–50; S. G. Strumilin, "The Economic Significance of National Education," in E. A. G. Robinson and J. E. Vaizey (eds.), *The Economics of Education* (London: Macmillan, 1966), pp. 276–323; Mark Blaug, "The Private and Social Returns on Investment in Education: Some Results for Great Britain," *The Journal of Human Resources*, vol. 2, no. 3 (Summer 1967), pp. 330–347; A. M. Nalla Gounden, "Investment in Education in India," *Journal of Human Resources*, vol. 2, no. 3 (Summer 1967), pp. 347–358; Marcelo Selowsky, "Education and Economic Growth: Some International Comparisons," unpub. diss., University of Chicago, 1967; G. S. Becker, "Underinvestment in College Education," *American Economic Review*, May 1960, pp. 346–354; Martin Carnoy, "Rates of Return to Schooling in Latin America," *Journal of Human Resources*, vol. 2, no. 3 (Summer 1967), pp. 359–374; Ruth Klinov-Malul, *The Profitability of Investment in Education in Israel* (Jerusalem: Maurice Falk Institute for Economic Research in Israel, 1966); also Giora Hanoch, "Personal Earnings and Investment in Schooling" (mimeographed), unpub. diss., University of Chicago, August, 1965.

[19] Harvey Leibenstein, "Rates of Return to Education in Greece," Development Advisory Service, Harvard University, Economic Development Report No. 94, September 1967.

merce and industry in the Athens area. The survey collected data on each worker's age, years of education (both technical and general), monthly earnings, and occupation. The sample included over 2,700 observations for the years 1964 and 1960.[20] He also used data on salary schedules for the workers in public service as well as information directly obtained from professional organizations. (It was found that the results of the sample survey were consistent with those directly obtained from both public and private organizations.)

Leibenstein computed both an internal rate of return and a net rate of return, defined as the net present value of the income increment minus direct costs as a fraction of the direct cost of education. While he emphasized the latter concept, in the interests of comparability with similar studies in other countries, I present his figures on the internal rate of return. (The internal rates of return and the net gain rate of return yield roughly the same qualitative results.) Column 4 of Table 17 presents the estimates of the internal rates of return based on the cross section of earnings in the survey.

Estimates of the age profile of earnings for a given individual based on a cross section of earnings will clearly be biased downward in the presence of a general productivity increase as a concomitant of economic growth. In view of the rather rapid rate of productivity increase in the Greek economy over the past fifteen years, Leibenstein has adjusted his internal rates of return upward by assuming that all earnings rise by either 4 or 5 percent per annum as a consequence of economic growth. The resulting rates of return are shown in columns 5 and 6 of Table 17.

All the estimates in Table 17 represent social rather than private rates of return in the sense that the full social cost of

[20] The survey was directed by Leibenstein with the assistance of A. Kallergie and the statistical staff of the Center of Planning and Economic Research in Athens. I am grateful to Professor Leibenstein for allowing me to use this data.

Alternative Approaches

Table 17. Approximate internal rates of return to years of education, assuming different rates of growth, Greece, 1960–1964

Years of education		Sex	Year of sample	Rate of growth (percent)		
				0	4	5
15 against 12		Male	1960	8.0	12.5	13.5
15 "	12	Male	1964	8.0	12.5	13.5
12 "	6	Female	1960	3.0	7.0	8.0
12 "	6	Female	1964	5.0	9.5	10.5
12 "	6	Male	1960	4.5	9.0	10.0
15 "	6	Male	1960	6.0	10.0	11.0
12 "	6	Male	1964	3.0	7.0	5.0
15 "	6	Male	1964	5.0	9.5	10.5

Source: Harvey Leibenstein, "Rates of Return to Education in Greece," Development Advisory Service, Harvard University, Economic Development Report No. 94, September 1967, p. 13.

schooling is counted in the calculations. Of course, they cannot be construed as social rates of return in a more general sense because of the very strong probability of a divergence between the social marginal productivity of each category of labor and its respective earnings. It should be further noted (as Leibenstein does in his paper) that these estimates take no account of the fact that some portion of the difference in earnings among workers classified by level of schooling must be attributed, not to schooling itself, but to other influences which are positively related both to the probability of acquiring additional schooling and to higher earnings in adult life. From the standpoint of social decision-making, one additional point should be made. The estimates in Table 17 refer to an individual who enters the indicated level of schooling, successfully completes the course, and, finally, both participates in and is successfully employed in the labor force over his entire life. Thus, in seeking an upper-bound estimate, Leibenstein assumed a pattern of scholastic progress and successful labor market participation which is rather atypical in the Greek educational system and economy. Wastage and retardation rates in secondary and higher education are high, and, moreover, labor force participation and employment rates are significantly lower than 100 percent (see Appendix 5). The estimates of the rate of return thus were not intended to represent the expected economic gain to society associated with the admission of a student to the level of schooling in question.

While the rate-of-return approach clearly does not yield estimates of required enrollment levels, Leibenstein feels that a number of policy decisions are implied: "Looking at education solely from the point of view of the creation of human capital, my tentative recommendations would be as follows: if the allocation is to be made out of the *fixed* educational budget then the direction of change should be from secondary education towards higher education or primary education."

Turning to the question of the optimal total resource availability of education, Leibenstein concludes that "it is unclear whether education *of the present quality* at the secondary and higher level *considered as a unit* can have any greater claims on an overall investment budget compared with other types of investment. The exceptions to this case would be the training for well-established professions such as engineering, chemistry, medicine, etc."

A LINEAR PROGRAMMING MODEL

The fourth and last method of educational planning to be considered is the intertemporal optimizing model of the educational sector. The model is identical to that outlined in the previous chapter; the system of equations appears in Appendix 3. The planning period was chosen so that it would be comparable to the fourteen-year period used by the Mediterranean Regional Project, 1961–1974.

Recall that the objective function for the model requires estimates of the present value of the stream of lifetime earnings associated with each level of schooling as well as of the present value of estimated direct costs. The lifetime earnings estimates were computed from the raw data from Leibenstein's sample of workers in the Athens area. The gross income stream associated with each level of education is a weighted average of the present value of expected earnings of dropouts, on the one hand, and of graduates, on the other. The weights here are the fraction of total admissions expected to drop out or to graduate. The expected earnings of both dropouts and graduates are a weighted average of expected male and female earnings, adjusted for unemployment and nonparticipation in the labor force. The foregone earnings-stream for a given type of school is the present value of the expected earnings of a graduate of the next lower level, adjusted by sex, unemployment, and labor force participation to correspond to a typical incoming student. The underlying data used for these adjustments are described in greater detail in Appendix 5. Data on direct current costs of schooling were based on information given by the Ministry of Economic Coordination as well as on data cited in the Mediterranean Regional Project's report on Greece. The available information on the opportunity costs of capital suggested that a discount rate of 10 percent was appropriate.[21] The resulting estimates of the objective function coefficients for the first year of the planning period appear in Table 18.

[21] This estimate was based largely on the marginal productivity of capital inputs in estimated production functions in manufacturing sectors. See "An Estimate of the Marginal Productivity of Capital in Greece," Appendix to: Samuel Bowles, "Sources of Growth in the Greek Economy, 1951–1961," Project for Quantitative Research in Economic Development, Harvard University Economic Development Report No. 20, April 1967.

Table 18. The present value of net benefits (1961 drachmas, discounted at 10 percent) associated with various educational activities in Greece in 1961 [a]

Activity	Present value of lifetime earnings	Present value of lifetime earnings foregone	Increment in present value of earnings (2) − (3)	Present value of direct recurrent social costs	Present value of net benefits (2) − (3) − (5)	Ratio of present value of increment in earnings to direct costs (4)/(5)
(1)	(2)	(3)	(4)	(5)	(6)	(7)
Primary	110,805	86,959	23,846	6,408	17,438	3.7
Gymnasium	196,845	115,083	81,762	5,623	76,139	14.5
Lower technical	220,959	164,043	56,916	36,011	20,905	1.6
Lyceum	200,425	189,784	10,641	5,623	5,019	1.9
University						
Humanities and social sciences	430,565	229,856	200,709	22,110	178,599	9.1
Mathematics and physical sciences	457,043	247,811	209,232	22,110	187,122	9.5
Engineering and related subjects	736,235	263,183	473,052	38,264	434,788	12.4

Source: See Appendix 5.

[a] Adjusted for expected future growth, wastage, failures, labor force participation, and unemployment.

Table 19. Annual capital costs per student place [a] and building costs per student place (drachmas), Greece, 1961

Type of building	Total cost per student place (C_k)	Total cost charged for building one student place in 1961 [b] (V_k^p)
Primary [c]	10,000	8,098
Secondary [c]	12,500	9,783
Lower technical [d]	46,500	37,670
Higher (humanities and social sciences) [e]	46,272	37,484
Higher (physical sciences and mathematics) [e]	60,511	49,023
Higher (engineering and related subjects) [f]	120,000	96,828

[a] All costs are exclusive of dormitories and other facilities not directly required by the education in question.

[b] See Chapter IV, equation (6), for a definition of V_k^p.

[c] Primary and secondary building costs are based on a detailed cost analysis of twenty-two construction components in buildings constructed during 1961–1963, expressed in 1961 prices. The basic data and analysis are in OECD, Development of Economy in Educational Building, *Preliminary Report*, No. 1, p. 10.

[d] Capital costs for lower technical schools are based on the actual costs of two new lower technical schools constructed in the period 1961–1963, expressed in 1961 prices. An addition of 25 percent has been made to account for equipment. See OECD, Development of Economy in Educational Building, *Preliminary Report*, tables VII and VIII. A third school for which data were available was considerably more expensive and was judged to be atypical. However, there is a distinct possibility that the capital costs figure for lower technical schools represents an underestimate.

[e] Costs for humanities, theology, law, physics, and mathematics are based on a report of the University Technical Service, "The Plan for the New University" (unpublished). Costs for pedagogical academies are assumed to be the same as the costs for humanities, theology, and law.

[f] The costs figure for engineering and related studies is based on unpublished plans for the new technical university of Athens.

The activities used in this model include primary school, gymnasium (first-cycle secondary), lyceum (second-cycle secondary), technical secondary education, primary school teacher training, higher education, both at home and abroad, and in the following three categories: humanities and social sciences, physical sciences and mathematics, engineering and related subjects.[22]

The initial teacher-student ratios and their projected movement over time were based entirely on the existing plans of the ministries of Education and of Economic Coordination, as reported in the Mediterranean Regional Project's report.

In addition to the activities representing school admission, a total of fifty-six activities were included to represent physical capacity creation, or, more specifically, school construction. The estimated costs for these activities were based on architectural plans and on estimates made by the Greek Government School Building Construction Organization and by an OECD team assigned to project costs of school construction. The capital cost per student place estimates used in the model appear in Table 19.

The estimates of the time profile of earnings and costs take into account the expected increases in costs per pupil due in part to increases in teacher-pupil ratios and an anticipated 3 percent per annum productivity increase.[23]

---

[22] Middle technical and Assistant Engineer Schools are not included here, as preliminary analysis of the data indicated that they would not appear in the optimal basis.

[23] The rate of 3 percent was chosen over Leibenstein's 4 or 5 percent on the grounds that the recent rapid productivity increase may not represent a long-term trend. The relevant adjustment is by a rate of labor productivity growth not due to increases in schooling, or the growth rate of Y/L°, when L° represents the quantity of labor services, adjusted for the educational composition of the labor force. The overall rate of growth of labor productivity includes the effects of changes in the schooling composition of the work force and therefore cannot be used to represent the upward shift of the demand functions for each category of labor taken separately. Over the period 1951–1961 the rate of labor productivity growth was 4.8 percent

Because of the large number of individuals in the Greek labor force in nonteaching jobs who possess the basic qualifications for teaching duties, activities which allowed the educational sector to recruit additional teachers were included in the model. These recruiting activities are particularly important in view of the large number of Greeks studying and working abroad who constitute a part of the potential pool of teachers. Recruitment requires a salary increment, which in this case is assumed to be paid to all teachers, not merely to those recruited. Thus, the unit cost of each recruiting activity is the *marginal*, rather than the average, cost. In every case the recruiting activity was constrained by an upper limit which was set equal to the number of teachers of each specification composing the initial stock of teachers in the year 1961, plus some fraction of the output of individuals possessing those qualifications throughout the planning period.[24]

The resulting system was composed of approximately four hundred fifty equations and two hundred twenty activities. The main results of the model in terms of the 1974 stocks of enrolled students and flows of student admissions are presented in Figure 24. Additional information on the optimal phasing of admissions appears in Figure 25.

The single most striking characteristic of the results is the rapid rate of growth of secondary education early in the planning period, followed by a significant expansion of higher education later in the period. The data on the present values of lifetime

---

per annum, of which only about one tenth of a percent per annum was attributable to the effects of schooling. These data suggest that the appropriate rate of labor productivity growth is 4.7 percent per annum. See Samuel Bowles, "Sources of Growth in the Greek Economy." Recurrent costs are projected to rise at about 7 percent per annum, although the actual rate differs among different types of schooling.

[24] The assumed fractions of output available for recruitment into teaching appear in Appendix 5.

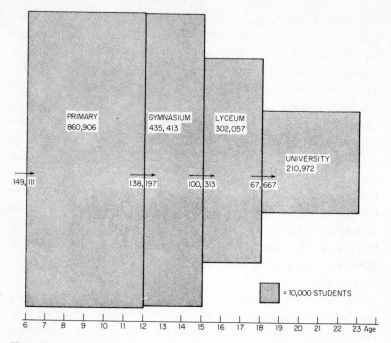

Fig. 24. Structure of the Greek Educational System, 1974, as Planned by the Optimizing Model

earnings and the costs of education (Table 18) establish a perhaps naive expectation that admissions to higher education will dominate the optimal solutions throughout the plan period. Yet the growth of higher education activities at domestic universities is heavily constrained by the scarcity of senior teaching personnel; the shadow prices of these resources early in the planning period are extremely high. Because of the significantly higher rate of attrition from foreign universities, these activities are also used at rather low levels in the early years.

A second major result is the change in the distribution of students within higher education. The behavior of the university enrollment variables in the last few years of the planning period

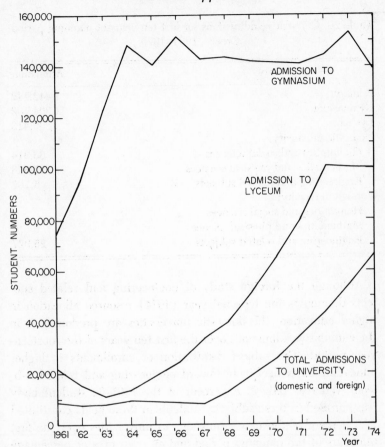

Fig. 25. Admissions to Greek Secondary Schools and Universities during the Planned Period 1961–1974

are heavily influenced by the specification of the terminal conditions,[25] which are necessarily somewhat arbitrary. For this reason we present cumulative admissions figures for only the first ten years of the planning period in Table 20.

[25] This is true in large part because some types of higher education produce intermediate goods (secondary school teachers).

Table 20. Cumulative admissions for first ten years of planning period: Greece, 1961–1970

Activity	Admissions
Primary	1,442,142
Gymnasium	1,304,786
Lyceum	290,413
Domestic university:	
Humanities and social sciences	65,914
Mathematics and physical sciences	15,548
Engineering and related subjects	5,702
Foreign university:	
Humanities and social sciences	0
Mathematics and physical sciences	0
Engineering and related subjects	25,927

Although the foreign study of engineering and related subjects dominates the terminal year (1974) resource allocation in higher education, the domestic universities are predominant in the cumulative admissions over the first ten years of the fourteen-year period. The subject distribution of enrollments in higher education shifts decisively toward engineering and related subjects. Whereas only 12.5 percent of the 1961–62 student body was enrolled in these subjects, students in these fields constituted 27.9 percent of the new admissions to universities over the first ten years of the planning period and an even greater percentage in the remaining four years. The relative distribution between the two remaining groups—mathematics and physical sciences, humanities and social sciences—is not significantly changed.

A third characteristic of the optimal solution can best be presented by looking at the continuation rates throughout the system for various years. It will be seen in Table 21 that starting from a position in which 46 percent of those leaving primary school entered the first-cycle secondary and only 45 percent of those

Table 21. Continuation rates in the Greek educational system in 1961
and as planned by the optimizing model for selected years

Level of schooling	1961	1968	1974
Gymnasium Admissions			
As a fraction of those entering			
primary school 6 years earlier	0.628	0.985	0.985
As a fraction of those successfully			
completing primary school	0.460	1.000	1.000
Lyceum Admissions			
As a fraction of those entering the			
gymnasium 3 years earlier [a]	—	0.282	0.711
As a fraction of those completing			
the gymnasium [a]	—	0.398	1.000
Admissions to Higher Education			
As a fraction of those entering the			
lyceum 3 years earlier [a]	—	0.728[b]	0.847
As a fraction of those completing			
the lyceum	0.450	0.859	1.000

Source: The Mediterranean Regional Project, *Country Reports, Greece*
(Paris: OECD, 1965), p. 54; table 7, p. 55; table 8, p. 57.

[a] Data on admissions to the gymnasium in 1958 and 1960 are not available.
Nor are data on 1958 lyceum admissions.
[b] Includes 2,756 in pedagogical institutes.

graduating from the lyceum achieved university entrance, we
move to a situation in 1974 in which all successful graduates of
a given level of schooling achieve entrance at the next level.
For the year 1974, therefore, we have positive shadow prices
relating to each of the equations which constrain the system not
to admit more students to any level than the number of available
students completing the next lowest level. These shadow prices,
as presented in Table 22, indicate the social costs (as measured
in terms of our objective function) of an individual's decision to
join the labor market rather than to continue his education at

Table 22. Shadow prices (drachmas) of graduates available for
admission to higher levels of schooling, Greece, 1961–1974

Year	Primary	Gymnasium	Lyceum
1961	0	0	0
1962	0	0	0
1963	0	0	0
1964	41,428	0	0
1965	38,343	0	0
1966	35,084	0	10,055
1967	32,994	0	0
1968	30,566	0	0
1969	64,504	0	7,719
1970	61,222	0	14,243
1971	58,446	0	41,023
1972	21,906	50,379	16,525
1973	24,261	49,647	15,888
1974	26,563	48,706	15,419

the termination of the type of schooling indicated. Thus, we
find that while the net benefits of study at the gymnasium level
(first-cycle secondary) are considerable (see Table 18), by the
end of the planning period, the derived demand for gymnasium
graduates as an input via the lyceum into higher education is
sufficiently great to make the maximum feasible continuation
rate optimal.[26]

The shadow prices in Table 22 are a measure of what Burton
Weisbrod has called "the financial option value" of schooling,
namely, the benefits of attending one level of schooling when
this level is looked upon as a prerequisite for attendance at a

[26] The notion of continuation rates going to 100 percent is not reasonable, particularly in a model with built-in wastage between most years of
schooling within a given course of studies. Given the high shadow prices
of continuing students, it is likely that some socially profitable program
could be devised to reduce wastage. Nonetheless, in any case one would
expect some wastage between, say, lyceum and university. A maximum
continuation rate (less than 100) could easily be imposed.

166

higher level.[27] Weisbrod discusses the value of the "financial option" in the context of the measurement of private rates of return to schooling. It is illuminating to note here that there is no social analogue to the private financial option unless the continuation ratios have reached their maximum feasible value, in this case 100 percent. Where there is a surplus pool of students from which to draw matriculants at each level, the shadow price of continuing students is zero, and while the private financial option is still relevant to individual decision-making, the analogous "social option value" is zero.

In view of the fact that the system of education is virtually inflexible by the terminal year due to the optimality of maximum continuation rates, the proper specification of terminal conditions becomes a matter of some importance. In specifying terminal conditions we attempt to do two things. First, we would like to achieve preterminal year production levels consistent with a desirable postterminal growth path. And second, we must correctly value the contributions of planned capacity expansion and the production of intermediate goods to postterminal output. The second point, though sometimes ignored in discussions of terminal conditions, is important if we intend to look at the shadow prices and other valuation aspects of the results as well as at the activity levels.

Without any terminal conditions on the model, no students would be admitted to the lyceum and some types of higher education in the years immediately preceding 1974. This phenomenon arises because students admitted to the lyceum in those years would not complete the course and therefore could not gain admission to a directly profitable activity, such as higher education, until after the end of the planning period. (Recall that the entire output of the lyceum is sent on to the university.)

[27] Burton Weisbrod, "Education and Investment in Human Capital," *Journal of Political Economy* (supplement), October 1962, pp. 106–124.

Moreover, the demand for some types of higher education is in large measure generated by the educational system itself. Students entering the university in the immediate preterminal period could not graduate and meet this demand for their services before the end of the planning period. Yet we can expect that the very strong indirect demand for lyceum graduates, derived from the economy's demand for graduates of higher education, will continue after the terminal year. And partly for this reason, the internal demand by the system for university graduates to teach in secondary schools will also continue after 1974.

In the application of this model to Nigeria, an analogous problem was solved by setting the preterminal year admissions levels in the affected activities at levels sufficient to generate postterminal growth in enrollments approximately equal to the rates of growth which were optimal during the planning period. This arbitrary restriction on preterminal activity levels was necessary because I took no account of the postterminal benefits associated with these activities; the postterminal services of teachers produced during the planning period were not valued, and the model took no account of the value of the students who remain enrolled at the end of the planning period. With no valuation of postterminal teacher services, in order not to over-count the cost of teachers, I ignored the costs of teacher training as well. As far as the cost and benefit accounting was concerned, production of teachers was outside the model: activities using teachers were charged a rent (salary) while the teachers were employed.

In a number of respects Greece was different, and required a different treatment. Unlike Nigeria, the major output of teachers in Greece is from unspecialized institutions which produce higher education generally.[28] The costs of production and the estimated

---

[28] Pedagogical academies constitute a minor exception. They admitted less than 10,000 students over the entire planning period. Because these activities produce only teachers, they were treated as in the model for Nigeria.

increment in lifetime earnings in the labor force outside of education constitute the objective function coefficients for these activities. The cost of using a university graduate as a teacher (withdrawing him from direct production) is his salary, which purports to be a measure of his social marginal productivity in alternative employment. Thus, as long as the shadow prices of teachers and market prices of university graduates coincide, no problem arises, as the post-terminal benefits associated with a university graduate have already been counted in the objective function. However, where the shadow price of teachers in the model considerably exceeds the estimated earnings of university graduates, the estimated stream of lifetime earnings of university graduates understates the contribution of university graduate teachers to national income.

The problem of valuing continuing students did not arise in the Nigerian case. Because continuation rates never reached 100 percent, no social option values arose, and the estimates of the increment in lifetime earnings provided an adequate measure of the postterminal benefits.[29] The pervasiveness of maximum continuation rates in the Greek case required explicit treatment of the social option value of the stock of continuing students.

The Greek situation thus required a more comprehensive treatment of the terminal conditions both for teachers and continuing students. I have placed an explicit value on the expected demands for intermediate goods and teaching capacity in the postterminal years. Thus modified, the objective function measures the contribution of students educated during the planning period, plus the value of the increase in the stock of productive capacity (teachers) as well as the goods in process (continuing students) in the terminal year. Having taken proper account of postterminal

---

[29] In the case of the Sixth Forms, continuation rates were generally high and often 100 percent. This single exception to the above statement was quantitatively insignificant, in part because the course is only two years long and, as a consequence, only one year's admissions were affected.

benefits, we do not have to impose any additional constraints on the preterminal activity levels.

In order to implement this approach, I needed a value of the continuing students based on the derived demand for future admissions to higher levels. Thus, rather than measuring only the direct demand for lyceum graduates (as measured in the net benefits coefficients of the objective function), I aggregated the direct and indirect demands. Fortunately, a simple measure of this sum is provided by the shadow prices of the maximum rate of growth constraints relating to the lyceum.[30] These shadow prices measure the increase in the present value of future national income associated with the admission of one additional lyceum student. Equivalently, the shadow prices measure the sum of the direct social net return to lyceum education plus the social option value of this type of schooling as a preparation for university admission. The value of the shadow price considerably exceeded the net benefits function for the lyceum activity in the same year; the derived demand for lyceum graduates (as inputs into higher education) was greater than the estimated direct demand for lyceum graduates in the labor market. The net benefits coefficients for the last three lyceum activities were replaced by a value based on this shadow price.[31]

A similar adjustment was made for higher education, although in this case the procedure was somewhat complicated by the fact that the outputs of higher education when used in the educational system are stocks, rather than flows. Thus, even the first year's activities contribute to the postterminal stock; some

[30] These constraints were active for a number of years before the end of the planning period. At the very end of the period, of course, they were not.

[31] Strictly speaking, a similar adjustment should have been made for the gymnasium. However, in view of the fact that this activity was run at its maximum value anyway, the slight underestimate of the total benefits was not serious enough to warrant changing the relevant coefficients. A similar argument applies to primary education.

valuation of the contribution to this stock had to be made in all years of the planning period. (The adjustments for the early years were very minor.) In this case the adjustment was made on the basis of the percentage of the output of each level going into teaching and the shadow prices of the appropriate type of teacher in the terminal year.

The new solution, with the correctly specified terminal conditions, closely resembles the initial solution without terminal conditions both with respect to activity levels and shadow prices. The relevant shadow prices in the new solution were very similar to those used in the specification of the terminal conditions; thus it was necessary to pursue only one iteration.[32] The lyceum and some types of higher education in the last four years of the planning period were run at levels higher than they were in the solution without terminal conditions. Activity levels in the first half of the planning period were not affected. Thus, the main impact of the incomplete specification of the terminal conditions seems to be confined to biases in the last four years of the plan, particularly with respect to the division of university students between domestic, as opposed to foreign, study and the composition of students among subject specializations.

Although I do not claim to have solved the problem of the correct specification of terminal conditions, the above approach is not only conceptually appealing but works well. Moreover, the use of the model sequentially on a continuing, year-to-year basis necessitates acting on only the first few years of each solution. In the policy-making context, the last ten years of the planning period can be considered the terminal conditions for the model. When viewed in this light, errors in estimation or

[32] Inspection of the simplex criteria in the optimal solution suggests that the optimal levels of the lyceum activity—which had gone to zero in the previous solution—are not sensitive to moderate variations in the valuation of the postterminal indirect demand for lyceum graduates. (No simple sensitivity test of this type was possible for the other activities.)

171

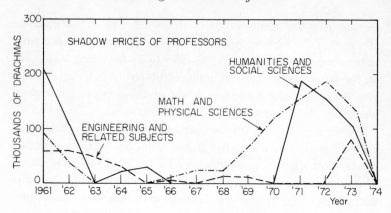

Fig. 26. Shadow Prices of University Professors in Greece,
1961–1974

other deficiencies in the specification of the terminal conditions
at the end of the fourteen-year period are apparently of little
importance.

Returning to the results, a fourth and particularly striking
aspect of the solution is that in no year of the planning period
is it optimal to admit students to secondary technical education.
This finding will be discussed in greater detail in the concluding
chapter.

A fifth important characteristic of the solution to the model is
the high productivity of resources in Greek education. The first
evidence is that the recruitment of teachers at salaries considerably above those currently being paid is found to be socially
optimal for virtually all types of teachers in all time periods. By
way of illustration, Figure 26 shows the shadow prices of university professors in humanities and social sciences, in engineering, and in mathematics and physical sciences over the entire
fourteen-year period. These figures represent the net increase in
the objective function above and beyond the normal teacher's
salary that is associated with having an additional teacher of

the type specified. The years characterized by very high shadow prices are those in which the activity recruiting these teachers into the system reaches its upper limit. In these years the shadow price can be thought of as comprising the social opportunity cost of withdrawing an additional teacher from directly productive activity, plus a rent on the upper limit on recruiting.

The high shadow prices of teachers suggest that programs of teacher recruitment from the labor force, including, if necessary, the payment of considerably higher salaries to all teachers, would be economically optimal. This is particularly clear in the case of teachers who possess the qualifications for teaching in universities. Programs designed to recruit Greeks overseas into teaching positions at home would appear to promise a considerable net economic return.

Additional evidence of the high productivity of the resources in Greek education is provided by the shadow price of expenditure on education. The solution of the dual indicates that every additional drachma of expenditure on education yields a net contribution to the present value of future national income of 1.6 drachmas. As this is equivalent to a benefit-cost ratio of 2.6 and a net rate of return of 160 percent on marginal expenditures, it seems safe to conclude that it would be economically rational to devote a higher level of expenditure to Greek education.[33] In view of the very high average productivity of expenditure —5.5 drachmas of present value of gross benefits per drachma of total expenditure—the high marginal returns are not surprising. Even if we assume that differences in schooling account for only 60 percent of the earnings differences among labor classified by educational level, the average productivity of expenditure in an optimal solution exceeds 3.2.

---

[33] Unlike the Nigerian model, the expenditure constraint here excludes foregone earnings of students in school. In both models foregone earnings are included in the objective function as a cost.

A Comparison of Results

The major differences in the results generated by the man-power requirements approach, the Tinbergen approach, the rate-of-return analysis, and the optimizing model can now be reviewed. Let us first summarize the results concerning the relationship of secondary to higher education. The Mediterranean Regional Project's application of the manpower requirements approach suggests that the admissions levels to both levels of secondary school should grow more rapidly than the admissions levels to higher education. In the solutions to the Tinbergen model, the rate of growth of secondary and higher education is identical. Recall that this is a direct result of the structure of the model itself. On the other hand, the rate-of-return approach suggests a more rapid rate of growth of higher education, although Leibenstein's work clearly does not recommend any particular rates of growth of admissions. The optimal solution of the linear programming model is characterized by very high rates of growth of secondary education early in the plan and by an expansion of higher education later in the period.

Second, the manpower requirements approach suggests doubling enrollments in secondary-level technical and vocational institutions over the period 1961–1974,[34] while the optimizing model suggests no admissions whatsoever to technical schools at the secondary level. Given the fact that the internal rate of return to secondary technical education exceeds 10 percent,[35] we may infer that the rate-of-return approach would recommend an expansion of this type of schooling.[36]

[34] Mediterranean Regional Project, *Country Reports, Greece,* p. 168.

[35] In Table 18 we see that the present value of net benefits of lower level technical education is positive, using a 10 percent discount rate.

[36] Leibenstein did not compute the internal rate of return for secondary technical education. Thus, this inference is based solely on my own analysis.

Third, the solution of the optimizing model suggests that it would be socially optimal to spend considerably more on education than the amount prescribed by the Mediterranean Regional Project in its application of the manpower requirements approach. The Project recommended an increase in total expenditure on education as a percentage of gross national product from 2.1 percent in 1961 to 3.2 percent in 1974.[37] Leibenstein indicated that the purely economic information provided no compelling economic reason for increasing the share of education in total resource use.[38] While no cost estimates were given for the solution to the Tinbergen model, Williams' results, using the modified demand function based on the international cross section, suggest that Greece already has considerably more than the "required" levels of educated labor.

There can be no doubt that different models give different answers—even when they use the same (or similar) data. In the concluding chapter I will relate some of these differences to the assumptions used in the various models.

[37] Mediterranean Regional Project, *Country Reports, Greece,* p. 192.

[38] As exceptions to this statement, Leibenstein lists training in engineering, chemistry, medicine, and similar "well established professions." The high shadow price in the optimizing model is in part due to the high marginal returns to the expansion of university activities producing at least some of these professions. Thus, the divergence between the results of the optimizing model and the rate-of-return approach may not be as serious as appears at first glance.

VI · Planning Models and Educational Policy: An Economic Evaluation

The choice of a set of assumptions is the central strategic decision in the construction of a policy model. The assumptions in large measure determine our data requirements, our computational needs, the kinds of questions we can hope to answer, and, sometimes, the answers themselves. It should come as no surprise, then, that four different models embodying varying assumptions about the nature of educational production and the demand for educated labor in the economy should yield radically different policy prescriptions for the allocation of resources in education. Experience from other countries suggests that the Greek case reported in Chapter V is not atypical. How can we explain these differences? (I will concentrate here on the Greek case, although I believe that much of the following material is more generally relevant.) Let me first summarize the differences in economic assumptions on which these methods are based.

THE CHOICE OF ASSUMPTIONS

The models are based on two fundamentally different ideas regarding the demand for educated labor. The conventional manpower requirements method and the Tinbergen approach conceive of demand in terms of the required numbers of workers, without reference to relative wages. In contrast, demand in both the linear programming model and the rate-of-return approach is measured by the differences in earnings among various categories of workers, without reference to the quantities of available labor. Strictly speaking, the demand functions in the requirements approach (both the conventional and Tinbergen versions) are totally inelastic; in the rate-of-return case and the linear programming model demand is infinitely elastic. Thus, the requirements approach corresponds to the "technological" case outlined in Chapter III, while the rate-of-return approach and the programming model correspond to the "economic" case.

Turning first to the manpower requirements method, the basic assumption is that the relationship between national income and level and distribution of schooling in the labor force is such that for a given level of future national income we are able to derive the number of workers at each level of schooling required by the economy. Following the procedure used by the Mediterranean Regional Project, this suggests that we must be able to: 1) determine the sectoral composition of output associated with any given level of national income; 2) within each sector determine the rate of growth of labor productivity; 3) within each sector determine the required occupational composition of the labor force; and 4) for each occupation determine a required distribution of educational attainments.

It is not made clear whether the occupational and schooling "requirements" in points (3) and (4) are to be understood as average or minimal requirements or as optimal distributions. In any case, the material presented in Chapter III suggests the difficulty in identifying either educational requirements for jobs or occupational requirements for sectors.

This is apparently a serious objection, as the economywide requirements of each type of labor, estimated on the basis of manpower studies, depend crucially on the choice of particular

Table 23. Labor skill distributions in Greece, actual and "required"

| | Actual | | 1961 "requirements," based on sectoral labor input coefficients of— | | | |
Skill level	1954	1961	Yugo-slavia	Portugal	Italy	Spain
Professional and managerial	2.12	2.57	5.12	1.51	2.50	4.10
High-level technicians	2.74	3.31	6.26	4.65	8.63	0.78
Skilled and semiskilled workers	38.73	40.43	43.44	29.28	18.44	42.19
Unskilled workers	56.41	53.69	45.18	64.56	70.43	52.93
Total	100.00	100.00	100.00	100.00	100.00	100.00

Source: George Psacharopoulos, "An Economic Analysis of Labor Skill Requirements in Greece, 1954–1965," unpub. diss., University of Chicago, 1968, pp. 73, 80.

sectoral occupational and educational input coefficients.[1] A recent study of manpower in Greece estimated the required stock of each type of labor in a model using five different sets of sectoral production technologies—those actually in use in Greece, Portugal, Spain, Italy, and Yugoslavia. The results, presented in Table 23, indicate that the required labor stocks in each skill category are extremely sensitive to even the limited range of substitutability represented by variations in the technologies of these five countries. If we take 1954 as the base year, we are not even able to determine accurately the sign of the required change in manpower supply.

Additional problems arise, for in an open economy it is hazardous to predict the commodity composition of output without reference to the factor endowments of the country. Yet step (1)

[1] See, for example, Robinson Hollister, *A Technical Evaluation of the First Stage of the Mediterranean Regional Project* (Paris: OECD, 1966).

in the manpower requirements method requires that we determine the sectoral distribution of output in order to plan how the educational system will be used to alter the factor endowments of the economy.

A further conceptual difficulty, as well as an additional empirical problem, is associated with step (2)—the prediction of future labor productivity trends. The underlying rationale of educational planning is that labor productivity is positively influenced by the level of schooling of the labor force. Yet step (2) demands that we predict changes in labor productivity in order to *determine* the level of schooling required in the labor force. Moreover, attempts to explain or to predict future labor productivity movements, even in advanced countries endowed with good historical series, have met with a conspicuous lack of success.[2]

The Tinbergen approach circumvents many of these difficulties, particularly those relating to occupational classifications and distributions, by directly estimating the relationship between income growth and level of schooling in the labor force. The estimated relationships (such as those used by Williams in his Greek study) are represented as *demand* functions for labor by level of schooling; in the original form, as estimated by the Netherlands Economic Institute, the equations are presented as representing "requirements" for labor of each type.

The fact that these estimates, which are based on a cross section of countries at one point in time, are intended to be used for a given country over a period of time raises some difficulties. However, there are two additional problems which are more fundamental and are common to the manpower requirements approach in either its conventional Mediterranean Regional Project form or its modified Tinbergen version.

[2] See particularly J. W. Kendrick, *Productivity Trends in the United States,* National Bureau of Economic Research (Princeton, New Jersey: Princeton University Press, 1961), pp. 113–189.

First, both methods use data on the observed level of labor input and the composition of the labor force by occupation or educational attainment. In the Tinbergen equation these values must be interpreted as optimal; otherwise, there would be no point in seeking to produce the "required" composition of workers. Likewise, when the future manpower requirements are based on the labor inputs of more advanced countries or of more advanced firms within the same country, the labor inputs coefficients in these technologies must be represented as optimal inputs. Yet these data on labor inputs are the consequence of a whole history of presumably suboptimal decision-making. If these quantities are not in fact optimal, then both methods will simply result in duplicating, or perhaps even exacerbating, existing scarcities and surpluses in the labor market.

But if the aggregate labor input data which form the empirical basis for Tinbergen's equations are optimal, must we conclude that the countries in his sample have no economic need for educational planning? Or that they have achieved this equilibrium of human capital and labor markets through the intelligent use of the available planning techniques? Were the countries in the sample chosen because they had an optimal labor force composition, and if so, how could this have been determined?

As long as we assume that private employers have some degree of technological choice, the observed input proportions—whether aggregate, as in Tinbergen's equations, or sectoral, as in the conventional manpower approach—will not be optimal, unless factor prices accurately reflect real scarcities. The only way to avoid this implication is to take literally the assumption that the elasticity of substitution among factors of production is zero, in which case the input proportions do not depend in any way on factor prices. Because this hardly seems tenable, I conclude that the use of observed technologies, whether best practice or average, relies on the assumption of factor market equilibrium and thus does not circumvent what is properly thought to be the main weakness of the rate-of-return and linear programming approaches.[3]

The central question here is the degree to which distortions in the factor market alter the results of these alternative approaches. This, in turn, depends on the degree to which factor input proportions are sensitive to relative factor prices. If the elasticity of substitution among factor inputs is high (as was suggested in Chapter III), a small distortion in relative factor prices will yield a much larger bias in the observed input proportions. Of course, the distortion in the quantitative results of these various methods depends on the empirical situation in which they are applied. Thus, although the above reasoning is suggestive, we cannot move directly from it to a preference for planning methods based directly on relative factor prices rather than on relative input proportions.

The second basic difficulty in both versions of the requirements approach comes from the impossibility of simultaneously identifying both the demand and supply functions for educated labor. The material in Chapter III suggests that educational attainments within occupations are determined as much by the labor supply as by the technical requirements of the job. Also, Tinbergen's "generalized demand equations" are equally plausibly interpreted as supply functions, in which the supply of educated labor is a function of the income level of the country. Thus, even if labor markets are in equilibrium, the data on labor inputs represent the intersection of a demand and a supply schedule; we are unable to distinguish whether the estimated "requirements" are determined by demand or supply.

[3] Of course, manpower requirements planners do have the option of using alternative technologies not based on observed market behavior, just as planners relying on the factor prices themselves can adjust them to account for known or suspected distortions.

Both the rate-of-return approach and the linear programming model are based on a fundamentally different assessment of the role of skills in the productive process. These two approaches rely on the assumption that the elasticity of the aggregate demand curve for each type of educated labor is sufficiently high that scarcities (as indicated by relative earnings in the base year of the planning period) can be used as a proxy for the expected degree of scarcity over a long period of time. These approaches assume that the labor market is in equilibrium, in the sense that the economy is operating on the aggregate demand function for each type of educated labor (as defined in Chapter III). It does not assume that the quantities of labor of each type are optimal, given the social opportunity costs of transforming labor from one level of schooling to another. Thus, both the rate-of-return and linear programming approaches assume equilibrium in the labor markets and are addressed to the task of achieving equilibrium in the human capital market, or more specifically, in the economic relations between the educational system and the economy.

Two problems immediately arise. The first is that we must question the degree to which wages of different categories of labor adequately measure scarcities. Second, even if the wage of each type of laborer were always equal to the value of his marginal product, we would still have to question the empirical assumption that the relative wages of labor do not significantly depend on the relative quantities of available labor.

Turning to the first problem, we know that the wages of any particular category of labor do not exactly measure the value of the marginal product. Wherever the demand functions facing firms are downward sloping or the supply of labor functions facing them upward sloping, we have reason to expect that wages will not equal the value of the marginal product. Moreover, even in perfectly competitive situations we often observe labor market disequilibria due to the sluggishness of the labor market adjustment mechanisms. Additional problems arise in countries like Nigeria where the government itself is the single largest employer of educated labor. The assumption that wages equal the value of the marginal product is particularly inappropriate in the government sector, not only because of the absence of explicit maximizing behavior in this sector but because of the impossibility of measuring the output of government services.

Of course, even if wages roughly measure the value of the marginal product for particular types of labor, we have no adequate way of estimating the portion of the increment in earnings associated with an additional year of schooling which can be attributed to the effects of schooling rather than to other factors.

The second major problem relates to the shape of the demand curve for educated labor. Data were introduced in Chapter III to suggest that a combination of direct substitution among labor of different levels of schooling and indirect substitution through changes in the composition of final demand resulted in a considerable amount of substitutability among the various types of labor. The constant elasticity of substitution labor aggregation function estimated in Chapter III, equation (15), allows the derivation of the aggregate demand function for each of three types of labor. We can use the labor aggregation function and the solution to the linear programming model for the Greek economy to test the empirical importance of the biases in our results likely to arise from my extreme assumption that demand functions are infinitely elastic. I will calculate the hypothetical earnings of each type of labor in the terminal year of the plan period on the assumption that the solution to the linear programming model has been implemented and the educational composition of the labor force altered accordingly. These hypothetical earnings are simply the marginal products derived from the labor aggregation function, using the hypothetical terminal year factor quantities. If the predicted earnings are very different from those estimated on the assumption that labor demands are

Table 24. Employed labor force in Greece:
actual 1961 and planned 1974

| Level of schooling | Fraction of labor force | |
(years)	1961 [a]	1974 [b]
0–7	42.4	29.8
8–11	47.1	57.2
12 or more	10.5	13.0
Total	100.0	100.0

[a] Samuel Bowles, "Changes in the Structure of Employment in Greece by Age, Sex, and Education, 1951–1961," Project for Quantitative Research in Economic Development, Harvard University, Economic Development Report No. 66, February 1967.

[b] Based on the solution to the programming model as described in Chapter V, corrected for labor force participation and unemployment.

infinitely elastic, our extreme representation of the demand for educated labor seems likely to seriously distort our results.

Table 24 presents data on the employed labor force of Greece in 1961 and on the employed labor force in 1974 based on the solutions to the model. The 1974 figures represent both the impact of retirements from the labor force and the effect of the educational plan prescribed by the linear programming model on new entrants to the employed labor force.[4] Despite the rapid expansion of particular types of schooling, the impact on the overall composition of the labor force is quite minor. This is a reflection of the limited degree to which the stock of labor can be transformed through formal schooling, given the rigidities of the educational system, and the small size of the annual flows onto the labor market relative to the size of the existing stock.

The objective function is based on net benefits. Thus an adequate sensitivity test must relate to differences in the earnings of various types of labor. The predicted changes in the differ-

[4] The 1974 figures are corrected for differential labor force participation and unemployment. See Appendix 5.

Table 25. Estimated effect of changes in labor force composition on the incremental earnings associated with additional schooling, Greece

	Percentage increases in the incremental earnings associated with additional schooling, 1961–1974		
		Predicted on the basis of the 1974 labor force composition if the model solution is implemented [b]	
Level of schooling (years)	Assumed in the model [a] ($\lambda = 0.03$)[c]	($\lambda = 0.03$)[c]	($\lambda = 0.047$)[c]
8–11, compared to 0–7	51.3	43.8	92.9
12 or more, compared to 0–7	51.3	52.2	93.0

[a] Based on the assumption that the demand for each type of labor is infinitely elastic.

[b] Based on Table 24 and equation (15) in Chapter III.

[c] $\lambda =$ the annual rate of labor productivity increase not due to schooling; the observed value of λ over the decade 1951–1961 was .047. Samuel Bowles, "Sources of Growth in the Greek Economy, 1951–1961," Project for Quantitative Research in Economic Development, Harvard University, Economic Development Report No. 27, April 1967.

ences between the earnings of two kinds of labor depend on the rate of growth of other factors and the rate of technological progress.[5] In Chapter V, I assumed, conservatively, that the impact of these influences on the growth of marginal products

[5] I assume a production function $Y = f(L^*, K)$ when L^* is the supply of labor services as defined in equation (15) in Chapter III, K and Y are capital services and output. Then,

$$\frac{\partial Y}{\partial L_i} - \frac{\partial Y}{\partial L_j} = \frac{\partial Y}{\partial L^*}\left(\frac{\partial L^*}{\partial L_i} - \frac{\partial L^*}{\partial L_j}\right)$$

The first term on the right depends on the level of non-labor factors (K) as well as the level of technology. I have termed its increase over time as the rate of labor productivity increase not due to schooling, or λ. Technical progress is assumed to be neutral with respect to the various categories of labor.

185

would be 3 percent per annum, although estimates based on Greek experience over the 1950's suggested a considerably higher rate. Table 25 presents estimates of the changes in earnings based on the labor force composition resulting from the educational plan generated by the model, using two alternative rates of labor productivity increase. If our original estimate of 3 percent was correct, we have slightly overestimated the returns to middle-level education. If the rate of productivity increase for 1961–1974 is equal to that experienced during the 1950's, we have underestimated the returns for both types of education measured here.

The results in Table 25 reinforce the finding that the return to resources in Greek education is high and suggest that biases resulting from my extreme assumptions concerning the demand functions for labor are comparatively minor.[6]

Of course, a more satisfactory test would be based on a disaggregated analysis. Unfortunately, the data on which the labor aggregation function is based cannot be extended to more than three factors. Marcelo Selowsky has performed a similar analysis of the impact of labor supply changes on relative factor earnings in Colombia.[7] Although he based his estimates on a comparatively low elasticity of substitution among six labor inputs ($\sigma = 3$), the internal rate of return to schooling was relatively insensitive to quite major changes in the composition of the labor force. For example, the estimated impact of a maximum politically feasible transformation of the composition of the labor force over a period of fifteen years was to lower the internal rate of return to primary school education from 28 percent to 24 percent. The

[6] Lack of the necessary labor force data prevented a similar sensitivity analysis of the Nigerian results.

[7] Marcelo Selowsky, "The Effect of Unemployment and Growth on the Rate of Return to Education: the Case of Colombia," Project for Quantitative Research in Economic Development, Harvard University, Economic Development Report No. 116, November 1968.

internal rates of return to all other types of schooling were even less sensitive.

To the extent to which the demand for labor is highly elastic, it is legitimate to plan future educational development by using existing labor market scarcities to evaluate the benefits of particular programs. However, if, as is quite likely in some cases, the capacity of the economy to absorb particular types of labor is rather limited, we would find that policy prescriptions based on existing scarcities might be inappropriate if carried to any considerable length over a period of time. The method, proposed in Chapter IV, of dealing with this problem was to treat educational planning as a continuing decision process, rather than as a single exercise, and to re-estimate and re-solve the model from year to year, using additional information as it becomes available. Thus, many labor market changes brought about by the operation of the educational system itself will be taken into account in the formation of educational policy in the later years of the planning period.

Enough has been said to suggest that the major differences among the four types of models are in the estimation of demand. Yet there are significant differences, too, in the representation of the educational system as a supplier of labor. The main differences relate to the way in which the cost of various programs is measured and the way in which the cost is related to the choice of educational policy.

The conventional manpower requirements approach is unique among the four methods in that it does not take costs explicitly into account. Educational requirements are determined from projected income levels without reference to the relative costs of the various types of educational production. This raises particularly serious problems when used in the evaluation of alternative educational programs for the creation of similar skills—for example, in the choice between formal education and on-the-job

187

training. Of course, the cost of the required level of educational enrollment was computed by the Mediterranean Regional Project's educational planners, but the requirements estimates were made prior to the cost estimates and therefore played no integral part in the establishment of the enrollment targets.

The cost of education in the rate-of-return approach is measured in money terms and is designed to take account of both the social and private costs of schooling. The basic assumption is that the market valuation of the school inputs is an accurate reflection of scarcities in the economy at large and that we are therefore justified in using the sum of the inputs into the program valued at their market prices as a measure of the social opportunity costs of the schooling.

Both the Tinbergen approach and the linear programming model measure costs in terms of physical inputs. Both explicitly represent the educational production process by a production function—using fixed teacher and student input coefficients. Thus, the outputs of educational programs are always net of the requirements of the educational system for its own inputs. Although the costs are also measured in money terms in the programming model, the opportunity costs of operating each activity in the model are based on the physical input coefficients relating to teachers and students and the shadow prices for these resources generated by the model itself.

In their treatment of educational inputs, then, the models fall into the "technological" and "economic" categories outlined earlier with respect to the input of educated labor in the economy. However, in this case it is the linear programming model and the Tinbergen approach which are distinctly "technological." [8] Differences among the models in their assumptions con-

---

[8] The manpower requirements approach is difficult to classify in this respect, but to the extent that school inputs are considered at all, it is within an "economic" framework.

Table 26. Classification of planning models according
to their fundamental assumptions

Assumptions with respect to the production of schooling	Assumptions with respect to the demand for educated labor	
	Technological	Economic
Technological	Tinbergen approach	Linear programming model (Chap. IV)
Economic	Conventional manpower requirements approach	Rate-of-return approach

cerning the production of education and the demand for
educated labor thus suggest a two-way classification scheme, as
is presented in Table 26. Obviously, the classifications are not
completely apt, but the taxonomy serves as a convenient summary of the above discussion.

The different treatment of costs in these models, as well as the
different concept of demand for educated labor, reflects two
fundamentally different approaches to economic planning. On
the one hand, the rate-of-return method and the programming
model are based on the principle of the maximization of national
income subject to constraints on resource use. On the other, the
manpower requirements approach and the Tinbergen model are
deterministic. They take as given a target of national income
growth and seek to derive from it a required level of educational
development. The educational plans resulting from these approaches are not intended to be optimal or efficient in the usual
economic sense of the words. This problem is particularly apparent in the conventional manpower approach, for, without reference to the costs of schooling or any explicit measure of the
benefits of hitting, as opposed to missing, the manpower targets,
we are unable to evaluate whether or not it is economically
desirable to achieve the "required" levels of schooling.

The choice of assumptions affects more than the formulation of the model; it directly determines the information requirements which must be met in order to use the technique in a given planning situation. In choosing a model for the education sector, the planner must select a set of assumptions which not only reflect the salient characteristics of his economy but which will also enable him to formulate the planning problem in such a way that the necessary data will be within his capacity to collect.

The chief difference in this respect between both of the manpower requirements approaches and the others is the level of aggregation. The Tinbergen model and the more conventional manpower requirements method require data on aggregate national income, population, and labor force classified by age and level of schooling. The conventional manpower requirements method requires information on the level of sectoral outputs (actual and projected) as well as historical data. In addition to this macroeconomic information, the manpower requirements approach requires data on the production technologies in the economy, with inputs disaggregated by occupation or level of schooling. The data requirements of the rate-of-return and linear programming methods are largely microeconomic: earnings, labor force participation, and unemployment, by level of schooling and age, the production technologies, or, alternatively, the costs of schooling, and, in the programming case, the supply of factors in the schooling system.[9]

Although much of the macroeconomic data is available in the rich countries, in the poor countries the required information is ordinarily either not available or subject to extreme error. In Nigeria, for example, there are no reliable estimates of the popu-

[9] Of course, all methods require much more data than these brief lists indicate. I have listed only those types of information which appear to exercise particularly great influence in determining the policy prescriptions of the models.

lation or of the labor force. Microeconomic data concerning the labor force are almost nonexistent. However, unlike the macro data, information on earnings by level of schooling and age (to take the most serious deficiency in the micro data) can be inexpensively and quickly collected on the basis of a sample survey. The required data on school production technologies and costs are ordinarily available. On the other hand, estimation of the aggregate quantities generally requires a more elaborate research strategy, and often a complete enumeration.

Of course, the accuracy of the microeconomic data from sample surveys may be very limited. This is particularly true when we estimate the difference between two earnings-streams, for in this case a small error in one stream may create a large error in the estimated present value of net benefits. For example, a 10 percent error in the estimate of the expected earnings-stream for graduates of the Greek gymnasium (without any offsetting error in the foregone earnings-stream) creates an error of over 20 percent in the estimated net benefits coefficient.[10]

In the Greek and Nigerian samples, the standard errors of the estimated earnings for each education/age group were quite large relative to the means. The large standard errors are due in part to the influence of stable characteristics such as ability or wealth, which suggests that errors in the stream of earnings and foregone earnings may be partially offsetting. Thus, it may be true that with a given set of information we can estimate the increase in earnings associated with an additional year of schooling with greater accuracy than we can estimate the level of earnings itself. But in any case the estimates are quite imprecise.

---

[10] More generally, recall that the variance of a difference between two randomly distributed variables (in this case the streams of expected earnings and foregone earnings) is the sum of the two variances minus twice the covariance.

THE CONSEQUENCES FOR EDUCATIONAL POLICY

The major divergences in the policy prescriptions of the four models can be explained by the differences in the representation of educational supply and the demand for educated labor as well as by the differences in choice between an optimizing and a deterministic approach. A survey of studies in a number of countries indicates that the divergent results fall into a pattern.

The Balance Between Primary, Secondary, and Higher Education

The manpower requirements school devotes little attention to primary education; their prescriptions tend to favor 'middle-level education.' Thus, Tinbergen's model assumes that labor with primary education or less is unlikely to be a scarce factor.[11] Similarly, Frederick Harbison, whose pioneering work constituted the origins of the manpower requirements approach, omits primary schooling from his measure of human resource development. In Northern Nigeria, a manpower requirements planning exercise prescribed gradual growth for primary education and a major expansion at the secondary level. The optimal solution of the linear programming model, on the other hand, was characterized by a decline in secondary school enrollment and an expansion of primary education at the maximum feasible rate. The internal rates of return implicit in the relative earnings data and the benefit cost ratios actually computed are consistent with the results of the programming model. Moreover, we find that in Uganda a study of the present value of the benefits and costs of primary, secondary, and higher education yielded policy prescriptions which differed substantially from those based on a

[11] Jan Tinbergen and H. C. Bos, *Econometric Models of Education, Some Applications* (Paris: OECD, 1965), p. 11; also, Frederick Harbison and Charles Myers, *Education, Manpower and Economic Growth* (New York: McGraw-Hill, 1964), p. 32.

manpower requirements approach.[12] Nicholas Bennett and John Smyth, using an approach involving the explicit measurement of the present value of benefits and costs recommended a major diversion of social resources from higher education to primary education. E. R. Rado and A. R. Jolly, using the Tinbergen approach, arrived at just the opposite conclusion, as have a number of applications of the manpower requirements approach. Estimates of the profitability of schooling for a number of countries (see Table 27) suggest a general predisposition of the rate-of-return method toward primary education, at least by comparison with the two versions of the requirements approach.

It is not surprising that optimizing methods which take explicit account of educational costs are more likely to find primary schooling a good investment than deterministic models which do not. When earnings foregone are taken into account, the data in Table 28 indicate that a year of general secondary schooling costs almost twice as much as a year of primary schooling in Greece and about twenty-two times as much as a year of primary schooling in Nigeria. The difference between the costs of higher education and primary schooling is, of course, much greater.

With respect to both Greece and Nigeria, the priority of secondary education in the conventional manpower requirements approach, as compared with the priority given primary or higher education in the rate-of-return or linear programming method, can be explained by the different assessment of the magnitude of demand for secondary-educated labor embodied in the models. In the Greek case, the Mediterranean Regional Project's conclu-

---

[12] See John Smyth and Nicholas Bennett, "The Rate of Return on Investment in Education: A Tool for Short Term Educational Planning Illustrated with Ugandan Data," in George Z. Bereday and J. A. Lauwerys (eds.), *The World Year Book of Education, 1967* (New York: Harcourt, Brace and World, 1967). See also E. R. Rado and A. R. Jolly, "The Demand for Manpower: An East African Case Study," *Journal of Development Studies,* vol. 1, no. 3 (April 1965), and Guy Hunter and F. H. Harbison, "High-level Manpower in East Africa: A Preliminary Assessment" (unpub., 1961).

Table 27. Profitability of schooling in various countries

| Country | Concept used | Date | Level of schooling | | |
			Primary	General secondary	Higher
Venezuela	Social internal rate-of-return [a] (percent)	1957	82.00	17.00	23.00
Chile	Social internal rate-of-return (percent)	1959	24.00	17.00	12.00
India	Social internal rate-of-return [b] (percent)	1960–61	17.00	11.00	8.00
Colombia	Social internal rate-of-return (percent)	1965	28.00	20.00	6.00
Mexico	Social internal rate-of-return (percent)	1963	25.00	17.00	23.00
Uganda	Benefit-cost ratio [c] $(i = 0.12)$	1965	3.70	2.70	0.99
Israel	Benefit-cost ratio $(i = 0.08)$	1957	3.48	0.71	0.29

Sources: Martin Carnoy, "The Cost and Return to Schooling in Mexico: A Case Study," unpublished Ph.D. diss., University of Chicago, 1964; Arnold C. Harberger and Marcelo Selowsky, "Key Factors in the Economic Growth of Chile" (mimeographed), presented to the conference at Cornell University on the "Next Decade of Latin American Development," April 20–22, 1966; Carl Shoup, *The Fiscal System of Venezuela* (Baltimore: Johns Hopkins Press, 1959), as reported in Martin Carnoy, "Rates of Return to Schooling in Latin America," *Journal of Human Resources,* vol. 2, no. 3 (Summer 1967), pp. 367–368; A. M. Nalla Gounden, "Investment in Education in India," *Journal of Human Resources,* vol. 2, no. 3 (Summer 1967), p. 352; J. A. Smyth and Nicholas Bennett, "Rate of Return on Investment in Education: A Tool for Short Term Educational Planning Illustrated with Ugandan Data," in George Z. Bereday and J. A. Lauwerys (eds.), *The World Year Book of Education 1967* (New York: Harcourt Brace, 1967), pp. 318–319; Ruth Klinov-Malul, "The Profitability of Investment in Education in Israel" (Jerusalem: The Maurice Falk Institute for Economic Research in Israel, April 1966), pp. 61–66; Marcelo Selowsky, "The Effect of Unemployment and Growth on the Rate of Return to Education: the Case of Colombia," Project for Quantitative Research in Economic Development, Harvard University, Economic Development Report No. 116, November 1968.

(*Footnotes on page 195.*)

Table 28. Opportunity costs [a] of a year of schooling at various levels: Nigeria and Greece

Level of schooling	Nigeria (1964–1965)		Greece (1961–1962)	
	Unit cost (£)	Unit cost compared to primary schooling	Unit cost (drs.)	Unit cost compared to primary schooling
Primary	10.7	1.00	2,417.0	1.00
Secondary general [b]	245.2	22.91	4,718.1	1.95
Secondary technical [c]	448.0	41.87	13,826.1	5.72
Higher [d]	902.0	84.30	15,363.3	6.36

Source: For Nigeria: Samuel Bowles, "The Efficient Allocation of Resources in Education, A Planning Model with Applications to Nigeria," unpub. diss., Harvard University, 1965, Chaps. 5 and 6. For Greece: Tables 18 and 19 and the sources cited there.

[a] Costs include foregone earnings and an annual capital charge based on the cost per student place multiplied by the rate of interest plus a depreciation rate. The depreciation rate is 0.03 in both cases; the interest rate is 0.05 for Nigeria and 0.10 for Greece.

[b] Secondary general refers to secondary schools up to but not including the Sixth Form in Nigeria, and to the gymnasium in Greece.

[c] Secondary technical refers to the technical training schools in Nigeria and to the lower-level secondary technical schools in Greece.

[d] Higher refers to university-wide costs in Nigeria, and to the costs for non-technical studies in Greece.

(Footnotes to Table 27.)

[a] In each case, the rate of return refers to the particular level of study only. Thus, the rates may be interpreted as marginal rates of return.

[b] The rate for secondary schooling is a simple average of the rates for middle school (11.8) and matriculation (10.2). The rate for higher education is an average of the return on a bachelor's degree (7.0) and an engineering degree (9.8).

[c] The benefit cost ratios were computed as the ratio of the present value of the earnings increment due to schooling to the present value of the direct costs of schooling. The discount rate is represented by i.

sions are based on its estimate that the occupations and sectors which are relatively intensive in the use of secondary-level labor are growing rapidly relative to other occupations and sectors. Yet if the high degree of substitutability assumed in the rate-of-return approach (as well as in the programming model) in fact obtains, then the structural changes which form the basis of the manpower requirements approach are unlikely to effect any substantial changes in current relative scarcities.

It may be that middle-level skills are likely to become increasingly scarce, but it is precisely these skills—particularly as compared with the skills associated with university education—which are readily learned through on-the-job experience, informal training, and other substitutes for formal schooling. Thus, the absence of choice in the production of secondary-level skills which characterizes the requirements approach may constitute a further explanation of the tendency of this planning method to prescribe comparatively rapid rates of growth for secondary school enrollments.

I believe that a similar analysis is sufficient to explain the differences in policy prescriptions among higher, secondary, and primary education found in the Nigerian and Ugandan studies.

The Phasing of Educational Development

The phasing of the conventional manpower requirements approach is ordinarily unspecified, although in Nigeria the prescribed patterns were simply constant growth paths. The rate-of-return approach specifies neither targets for enrollments nor paths of growth. In both the Greek and the Nigerian studies the programming model yielded a somewhat unexpected optimal pattern of growth in enrollments—the postponement of expansion of the most highly profitable activities till late in the period pending the development of capacity in these sectors and the sectors supplying them with inputs.

The linear programming model clearly reveals the "capital structure" of the education system. A number of types of schooling—sometimes only one, as in Nigeria—are chosen as the most profitable means of producing "labor services" for employment outside the educational system. Higher education in Greece and primary education in Nigeria are in this category of final goods. The remaining activities in the system deliver their outputs to these final sectors in the form of intermediate goods and capacity creation. The capital goods sectors ordinarily expand early in the period, with the expansion of the final goods sectors coming later. Both the Greek and the Nigerian solutions (as well as the mathematical structure of the problem) suggest that if run over a long enough period, the linear programming model would choose an optimal growth path in which the number of sectors delivering labor to employment outside education would be equal to or less than the number of exogenous constraints.[13] This path would be analogous to balanced expansion in a linear growth model of the von Neumann type. As the exogenous constraints include the boundary conditions as well as the primary factors (school-age children and expenditure), the number of activities making positive deliveries to the labor force might still be rather large.[14]

Much more interesting, from the comparative standpoint, is the distinctive phasing of educational expansion which is evident in the solutions of the optimizing model. In the Greek case, the early expansion of gymnasium admissions, followed by the expansion of lyseum admissions, and, finally, by the expansion of admissions to institutions of higher learning, appears to reflect

[13] I am ignoring unintentional deliveries through wastage.

[14] Although these speculations are of some interest from the standpoint of the theory of planning, they should be of no relevance in practice. In the first place, there is no reason to operate these models over extended periods as long as they can be operated sequentially. And second, the assumption of linearity in both the production and demand relationships becomes implausible when a single model is operated over a twenty- or thirty-year period.

the existing bottlenecks in the system as well as the social profitability of the various educational activities. I have commented earlier on the economic plausibility of the unexpected optimal phasing of Nigerian primary education. In this respect, the results of the programming model point up the strengths of a highly disaggregated intertemporal approach which takes explicit account of the short and medium range phasing of enrollment increases in the context of a maximization problem subject to the internal productive structure of the educational sector.

General versus Technical Education at the Secondary Level

Equally revealing of the differences among the models is the case of technical education at the secondary level. The manpower requirements approach seems to yield rapid required rates of growth of this type of schooling, and it is partly for this reason that in many parts of the world, technical education is regarded as the prime, if not the only, contribution of education to economic development. Solutions to the linear programming model in both Nigeria and Greece suggest a diametrically opposite view.[15] Applications of rate-of-return or benefit cost criteria in Greece, Nigeria, and Colombia indicate that the social profitability of secondary technical education is low relative to general education.[16]

Recall that the Mediterranean Regional Project recommended a very rapid rate of growth for Greek secondary technical education. On the other hand, the optimal solution to the intertem-

[15] A considerably more comprehensive analysis of vocational training in Ghana arrives at conclusions critical of the current government plans, which were based on a requirements approach. See Philip Foster, "The Vocational School Fallacy in Development Planning," in C. A. Anderson and M. J. Bowman, *Education and Economic Development* (London: Frank Cass and Co., 1966), pp. 142–166.

[16] See Chapters IV and V, and Guillermo Franco Camacho, *Rendimiento de la Inversion en Educacion en Colombia* (Bogota: CEDE, Universidad de los Andes, 1964).

poral planning model showed no admissions to secondary technical schools. This may appear somewhat surprising when we recall that the internal rate of return on resources devoted to lower-level secondary technical education exceeded 10 percent; the present value of net benefits per admittee to this type of school (using a 10 percent discount rate) is 20,905 drachmas.

The discrepancy between the rate-of-return and linear programming approaches arises because of a difference in the treatment of school costs and inputs—"economic" in one case, "technological" in the other. The economic approach to the production of schooling embodied in the rate-of-return method fails to take account of the distinction between market costs and the real social opportunity costs of educational inputs, as represented by the shadow prices in the optimal solution of the linear programming model. In the case of secondary technical education, the only two inputs explicitly considered are primary school leavers and expenditure itself. Throughout most of the period the shadow price for primary school leavers in the optimizing model is positive (see Table 22), indicating that the social opportunity costs of using primary school graduates for admission to technical schools is greater, and sometimes considerably greater, than the lifetime earnings-stream which appears as a cost in the objective function of any activity using these graduates as an input. For this reason the cost of admitting primary school leavers to any activity is understated by market prices. The direct demand for these graduates in the labor market is exceeded by the derived demand for primary school graduates as intermediate goods in the production of higher levels of education. This particular divergence between social and market costs is not captured in the present value calculation or by the implied internal rate of return, although it is fully accounted for in the explicit representation of interaction between educational activities which constitute the constraint equations of the optimizing model. This is why the lower-level secondary technical schools proved to be socially unprofitable in the optimizing model, despite their apparent profitability as measured by the present value of net benefits.

The failure of secondary technical schools to admit students even when primary school leavers are abundant—as in the first few years of the planning period—is explained by the fact that expenditure itself is a major input into technical education, and, as noted above, the shadow price of expenditure is considerably greater than one. When we devote social resources to the production of secondary technical education we must withdraw them from other educational pursuits on which the social returns are considerably higher. Thus, for example, if we re-evaluate the data in Table 18, using the social opportunity cost of expenditure rather than the market cost, we find that the net benefits per admittee to the lower secondary technical schools are negative.[17]

The divergence between the rate-of-return and linear programming methods concerning the profitability of Greek technical schooling provides an illustration of the advantages of a technological approach to the production and cost aspects of the educational planning problem.

The differences between the prescriptions of the Mediter-

[17] Because the objective function measures *net* benefits, the opportunity cost of expenditure on technical education (namely, the gross benefits foregone elsewhere per unit of cost) is one plus the shadow price of total expenditure. The social net benefits of technical education are then the present value of the earnings increment, minus the opportunity cost of direct expenditures, or (from Table 18) $56,916 - 2.6(36,011) = -36,713$ drs.

If the level of aggregate expenditure on education were increased until the marginal net productivity of additional expenditures were zero (shadow price = zero), the real social opportunity cost of a drachma of expenditure would be only one drachma. In this case secondary technical education would appear in the optimal solution, at least for those years in which primary school graduates are abundant. At more nearly optimal levels of expenditure on education, the divergence between the rate-of-return and linear programming results would probably disappear.

ranean Regional Project and the programming model are considerably easier to understand. Although both approaches indicate a substantial demand for graduates of secondary technical institutions, the lack of consideration given the particularly high cost of technical education in the manpower requirements study has led to an overstatement of the economic value of this form of education.[18] (See Table 28 for a comparison of unit costs of technical and other types of schooling.)

The difference in results given by the requirements approach and the programming model is heightened by the treatment of the acquisition of vocational skills outside the formal schooling system. A secondary school graduate or dropout may acquire technical skills through on-the-job training or from learning by doing, as well as in technical schools. These opportunities are implicitly recognized in the programming model. In the requirements approach, however, it is generally assumed that each technical skill corresponds to a single formal schooling process. Thus, this method allows no choice among the various means of acquiring skills; indeed, it could not without explicit consideration of the relative costs of various methods.

Thus, although the difference in results stems in part from the failure of the requirements approach to deal with the costs of schooling, it is also due to the greater degree of choice implicit

[18] There is one possible source of bias operating against secondary-level technical education in the rate-of-return and linear programming models. If the student selection process results in the more able or socially favored children attending general secondary schools rather than technical institutions, we have overestimated the relative profitability of general education by charging these two different groups of students the same foregone earnings-stream. However, the failure of technical schools to appear in the optimal basis in both the Nigerian and Greek studies could not be due to any error of plausible magnitude from this source or to simple errors in estimation. For example, in the Greek case, in most years of the planning period, the objective function coefficient for technical secondary schooling could be more than tripled without altering the optimal solution. The Nigerian solutions were even more insensitive.

in the programming model and to the fact that in at least these two cases the optimal path to middle-level vocational skills does not pass through the existing formal schooling system.[19]

Apparently, technical education at the middle-level is likely to be a particularly bad investment in poor countries characterized by small manufacturing sectors and a high rate of return on human capital investment generally. The costs of training are likely to be high, in part because of the scarcity of the high-level skills required in the teachers, but also because of the relatively small number of students enrolled in each course of studies and the resulting underutilization of the expensive and specialized teaching staff and physical capital of the school. Further, the opportunity costs of the entire range of inputs—students as well as general teachers—are likely to be considerable due to the high level of derived demand for their services in other types of schools.

The Level of Expenditure on Schooling

The last major divergence among these models concerns the optimal levels of expenditure on formal education. In both Greece and Nigeria the linear programming model suggested an expansion of the educational sector considerably beyond the levels prescribed by the requirements studies. The conclusions of the rate-of-return study in Greece are probably closer to those of the manpower requirements studies, while it is safe to say that a rate-of-return study in Northern Nigeria would recommend a considerable increase in expenditure on education. This can

[19] The nonoptimality of technical schooling at the secondary level is not a general characteristic of linear programming solutions, however. James Huntsberger, in his linear programming study of Canadian education, found that a considerable expansion of technical education at the secondary level was optimal. See James R. Huntsberger, "The Efficient Allocation of Resources in Canadian Education," Project for Quantitative Research in Economic Development, Harvard University, Economic Development Report No. 103, July 1968.

hardly be called a difference in results; it is, rather, a difference in the questions asked. For neither the manpower requirements approach nor the rate-of-return method seeks to determine an optimal total expenditure on education. The requirements approach, in fact, precludes such a question, for if we are to interpret the "requirements" literally, there is only one educational plan consistent with each rate of growth of total output; thus the question reduces to finding the optimal growth rate. Alternatively, if the manpower requirements are given a more common sense interpretation, we have no idea of the economic consequences (either benefits or costs) of exceeding, falling short of, or exactly meeting a requirement; thus there can be no question of the optimal level of expenditures. In any case, my linear programming model indicates that there are significant economic returns to levels of expenditure on education above and beyond those prescribed by the estimated manpower "requirements" of the labor force.

In theory, the rate-of-return method allows an estimate of the optimal total expenditure on education. We could begin by listing all types of schooling in descending order of internal rate of return and then expanding the most profitable activity to its maximum feasible level consistent with the internal structure of the system, the total available resources, and any other exogenous constraints. Proceeding down the list to continually less profitable activities, one would finally come to one whose profitability fell short of that on available investments in the rest of the economy. No expenditure on this activity would be independently justified (although it might be used as an input elsewhere), and the resulting amount of expenditure on all the included activities would be optimal. Alternatively, if the educational system is operating with a fixed constraint on total expenditure, then the profitability of the last included category of educational expenditure is a measure of the marginal productivity of resources in education. Of course, endless iterations would be needed to achieve internal consistency in the system, and, in any case, the resulting solution would be similar to that achieved with the programming model through a much simpler procedure. In fact, the computational method for the solution to the programming problem closely corresponds to the method just described, with the important difference that the profitability of each educational activity is evaluated on the basis of shadow prices generated by the system itself rather than on the basis of market prices.[20]

All four approaches to educational planning are subject to serious error and have required in their construction a number of assumptions of dubious validity. None is without redeeming features. A brief overall evaluation is now in order.

The existence of bottlenecks and rigidities within the educational system has demonstrated the importance of using explicit production functions for the educational activities to represent the structure of the educational production possibility set. Exclusive reliance on money measures of inputs has been shown to be seriously misleading as to the real costs of educational production. In this respect the Tinbergen model and the linear programming model are clearly superior to the other approaches. The degree of disaggregation of the educational production system made possible by the programming model and the resulting close correspondence between the variables in the model and the actual policy instruments strongly recommends it over the Tinbergen approach, which is effectively limited to a small number of distinct types of labor.[21]

---

[20] The simplex criterion, which is used to determine which activities are to appear in the solution of a linear programming problem, is a measure of an activity's gross contribution to the value of the objective function, minus the opportunity costs of the activity's inputs, valued at their shadow prices.

[21] The assumption that at any given income level labor categories cannot be substituted becomes increasingly implausible as the number of types of labor increases.

Evaluation of the treatment of the demand for educated labor is more difficult. On one crucial empirical issue, the elasticity of demand for factors of production, the evidence presented in Chapter III seems strongly to support the assumption underlying the rate-of-return analysis and the programming model. The zero substitutability assumed in the two versions of the requirements approach seems completely untenable, even as a rough approximation. However, the rate-of-return analysis and programming model require more than a high elasticity of demand; correspondence between earnings and social marginal product (to name only the most central assumption involved) is also necessary. On this question the evidence is far less compelling. Whether the assumption is useful depends on how sensitive the results are to plausible divergences between the real world and the assumed one. In both the Nigerian and Greek cases the principal findings were not sensitive to small variations in the parameters, although a thorough analysis of the effects of all possible combinations of errors was never attempted. A particularly desirable feature of the programming model is the ease with which this sensitivity analysis can be carried out.

Thus, although we must await other applications before general confidence can be placed in the intertemporal linear programming model, conceptual considerations strongly recommend it, and the initial experience in two countries has produced encouraging results.

Having stressed the differences among the four approaches, let me conclude this comparison of models by suggesting that in many respects the methods are complementary. The practitioner of the manpower requirements approach can, of course, make good use of rate-of-return studies, or of a linear programming model, in determining the optimal methods of producing amounts of labor which are thought to be required. Where the results of rate-of-return studies or optimizing models diverge substantially from the estimated requirements, the planner may decide to revise his target levels of enrollment in order to introduce a kind of informal optimization into the requirements approach.[22] On the other hand, no planner using the rate-of-return approach or the programming model can afford to ignore the sort of information generated by the usual manpower requirements study. For it is precisely this information which allows us to make intelligent guesses about the future shifts in the demand curve for educated labor. In an economy with imperfectly functioning markets—and one which is moreover undergoing particularly rapid structural and technological change—a combination of approaches is preferable to any single method.

THE IMPORTANT QUESTIONS UNASKED

In closing, at least three major shortcomings of my model deserve comment, for it is in these areas that I believe the most fruitful advances in future model building can be made.

The first is the inadequate representation of the educational production processes. While the use of existing and anticipated marginal input coefficients is probably a reasonably good reflection of the techniques actually in use or likely to be introduced, the application of planning models to questions of the choice of educational technique would be greatly assisted by a more precise knowledge of the relationship of teacher quantity and quality, school facilities, student social class, and other input measures to the various dimensions of the educational output.[23] Particularly

[22] For a complete development of this iterative procedure, see George Psacharopoulos, "An Economic Analysis of Labor Skill Requirements in Greece, 1954–1965," unpub. diss., University of Chicago, 1968.

[23] A number of economists and other social scientists are currently working on this problem. See Samuel Bowles, "Towards an Educational Production Function," paper presented to the Conference on Education and Income of the National Bureau of Economic Research, November 1968, and the references cited therein.

important in this respect is the development of a more adequate understanding of the process by which schooling renders individuals more productive.

A second major shortcoming of the model is due to its sectoral nature. A more general model of the entire economy, in which the demands for the outputs of the educational system are generated endogenously rather than estimated exogenously, can easily be conceived. Such a model would allow the supply functions for all educational inputs to be endogenous as well. The chief advantage of this approach is the possibility of incorporating less extreme assumptions concerning the nature of the demands for educated labor, and allowing the allocation of resources in education to be determined by direct estimates of the productivity of labor, generated from the optimal pattern of growth in the economy. The chief difficulty lies in the data requirements and computational complexity of a disaggregated economywide model in which the relations between labor demands and sectoral outputs are even slightly more complicated than those presented in this study. Considerable work is already under way in this area.[24]

The remaining problem is at once the most important and the most intractable: we have ignored the consequences of alternative educational plans for the distribution of income. This shortcoming is important because we desire social justice as well

[24] See especially Irma Adelman, "A Linear Programming Model of Educational Planning: A Case Study of Argentina," in Irma Adelman and Erik Thorbecke (eds.), *The Theory and Design of Economic Development* (Baltimore: The Johns Hopkins Press, 1966), pp. 385–411. See also Christopher Dougherty, "A Prototype Planning Model for the Efficient Allocation of Resources in Education" (mimeographed, 1968); Jean Benard, "General Optimization Model for the Economy and Education," in OECD, *Mathematical Models in Education Planning* (Paris: OECD, 1966), pp. 207–244; Frederick L. Golladay, "A Dynamic Linear Programming Model for Educational Planning with Application to Morocco," unpub. diss., Northwestern University, August 1968; and Marsha L. Geier, "An Educational Planning Model for Chile," unpub. diss., Northwestern University, August 1968.

as a large gross national product, and there is no reason to expect that the pattern of educational development which maximizes the rate of economic growth will at the same time generate an equitable distribution of income. The problem is intractable because it can neither be reduced to a form solvable in the present computational context nor can it be analytically separated from the question of efficient resource allocation in education.

This intractability arises because I have used the market earnings of each type of labor as the basic data for the objective function. Because the demand for factors of production is derived from the demand for the commodities which they produce, the payment to factors is dependent on the market demands for goods and services. These demands, in turn, depend on individual tastes and the distribution of income. Thus, the existing distribution of income is built into the objective function with which we seek to evaluate the optimality of various paths of educational development. A more equal distribution of income would give us a different maximand and, presumably, a different "optimal" pattern of educational development.[25]

Thus, although we have no idea of the quantitative significance of this relationship between the existing distribution of income and our "optimal" pattern of enrollments, we would be defeated at the start if we sought to separate considerations of

[25] Of course, the consequences of this new solution would not necessarily be more egalitarian than the first solution; for that to be the case, luxury goods would have to be intensive in the skills possessed by the rich, and vice versa. The magnitude of the difference in objective functions estimated from factor prices based on different income distributions will depend in part on the degree to which the technologies of various sectors differ in the intensity with which they use each type of labor input and on the differences in the income elasticities of demand for various goods. If the income elasticity of demand for all goods were one, or if there were no differences in the skill intensities of sectors of the economy, this problem would not arise. What is really crucial here is the existence (or lack of it) of a consistent relationship between the skill intensity of a sector and the income elasticity of demand for its products.

efficiency and equity. For if we were to accept the view that we should maximize national income according to the prescriptions of our model, and solve the distributional questions later, we would find that the income distribution at the end of the planning period, either before or after redistribution, would differ from that upon which our original definition of "optimality" and national income was based.

Faced with these conceptual hurdles, there are three possible courses. First, we could ignore the problem altogether. Alternatively, we could clarify the distributional consequences of each plan so as to allow, or even encourage, educational policy makers to weigh these issues along with those of economic efficiency in choosing an educational plan. Last, we might ignore the above warnings and attempt to incorporate income distribution objectives directly into the planning model, knowing in advance that the attempt could at best be only partially successful. Having followed the first course throughout most of this study, I turn now to the other two alternatives.

We are interested in the impact of educational decisions on the distribution of expected lifetime labor earnings. Thus, I will not deal with income inequality that is due to the ownership of non-labor factors, such as land and capital, or with that arising from the normal variations in earnings over the life cycle. The data on the expected lifetime earnings of labor with a given level of schooling which form the basis of the objective function also allow the calculation of the effects on income inequality of a given solution to the programming model.[26]

Recall that in the solutions of the model for Greece, primary education is universal, and gymnasium education nearly so. Thus,

[26] If we had a more detailed breakdown of the labor force by years of schooling in the base year, we could calculate a number of convenient summary measures of equality, such as the Gini concentration ratio based on the Lorenz curve of income.

implementation of the model's prescriptions would greatly reduce the size of the lowest segment of income earners, those with less than a primary education. As a result, the percentage of total life-time earnings earned or expected by the bottom third of income earners would be somewhat increased (from 22 to 25 percent) by the implementation of the solution to the model. On the other hand, the top 10 percent of income earners are expected to earn about 21 percent of total lifetime earnings both in the base year and in the hypothetical 1974 situation based on the programming solution.[27]

The quantitative effects of alternative educational plans on the distribution of income in Nigeria are somewhat more difficult to assess, as we lack data on the total population or work force by level of schooling. Nonetheless, it is clear that the strong emphasis on primary education prescribed by the linear programming model has the effect of reducing income disparity, because it moves individuals from the lowest earning category to a level of schooling associated with about average earnings. For analogous reasons, the Nigerian government plans are inegalitarian in their probable impact, at least by comparison with my solutions, for they concentrate on transferring individuals from a level of schooling slightly above the mean to skill levels associated with the top quartile of income earners.

The harmony of distributional and growth objectives suggested by my model is entirely fortuitous. In some models, however, the distributional biases are predictable. For example, methods which do not regard primary school graduates as a scarce factor of production (such as Tinbergen's) or those which do not take account of relative schooling costs (such as the conventional

---

[27] These estimates are based on the highly aggregated data available and do not reflect the dispersion of income within these labor force aggregates; it is assumed that each individual in a given schooling category earns the expected earnings associated with that category.

Planning Models and Policy

manpower requirements approach) contain an intrinsic bias against primary schooling which leads to educational policies which are likely to be not only inefficient but inegalitarian as well.

To build distributional biases into a planning model is much more difficult than to detect their inadvertent appearance in models whose architects claim no interest in these questions. However, if the concept of equality which we seek is adequately represented by a reduction in the dispersion of expected lifetime earnings, we can proceed as follows. As it is presently formulated, the model implies a set of distributional preferences which can be expressed in the statement: the social value of a dollar increase in lifetime earnings does not depend on the expected income level of the recipient. A dollar to a rich man has the same value to society as a whole as a dollar for a poor man. Let the distributional preferences of the planners be represented by a function which measures the social welfare E derived from the income, Y, of each class of income recipients, here grouped by years of schooling. The preference function implied by the objective function as it now stands is $E = Y$. For the sake of illustration, I now give the planners the following egalitarian preference function, $E = \log Y$. In this case, for example, a dollar increase in the income of an individual expecting to earn $10,000 in his lifetime is twice as socially valuable in the planner's eyes as the same income increase to a person expecting $20,000. The crucial attribute of this preference function is that the marginal social utility of income is a declining function of the amount which the recipient can expect to earn.

In my model each potential admittee to a school is classed by the level of his expected lifetime earnings. Thus, it is a simple matter to inncorporate a rough measure of preference for equality into the analysis by recalculating the objective function using the above planner's preference function.[28] The original coefficients and the recalculated egalitarian objective function for both Greece and Nigeria are presented in Table 29. The results are predictable. The lower levels of schooling are uniformly more socially profitable, while the upper levels are less so. Thus, the introduction of egalitarian objectives into my Nigerian model would considerably strengthen the findings concerning primary education. In the Greek case, the growth-maximizing pattern of enrollments would probably remain 'optimal,' the most rapid development possible of each part of the system starting from the bottom up.

A model based on this approach—perhaps using a range of planner's preference functions—could easily be constructed. While the shortcomings are many, and obvious even at this abstract level of development, such a model should be a top priority research task for economists and educational planners. For the notion that the issues of equity and efficiency can be separated is far more dubious than purely economic-theoretic reasoning would suggest.

The economic consequences of schooling are in large measure embodied in human beings, and the income distribution within a society is an outcome of the distribution of these built-in skills and capabilities. Given the limited ability or willingness of most societies to use the fiscal system as a means of redistributing income in any significant way, the idea that the economist's role is to maximize income while leaving the distributional issues to the politicians serves as a rather transparent rationale for ignoring distributional issues altogether. The idea that these two fundamental issues—efficiency and equity—can be segregated is

[28] I have arbitrarily weighted the cost of direct educational expenditures as if they were raised in taxation from secondary school graduates in Nigeria and gymnasium graduates in Greece. Each individual is treated as an income earning unit—obviously an unrealistic assumption, given the tendency of school children to grow up and get married.

Table 29. Net benefits of educational activities with egalitarian planners' preferences: Nigeria (1964) and Greece (1961)

Activity	Present value of lifetime earnings of potential admittee [a] (£'s and drs.) (1)	Marginal social utility of income for this class of admittees (egalitarian preferences) [b] (2)	Net social benefits (egalitarian preferences), [c] in £'s and drs.) (3)	Net social benefits used previously in model [d] (£'s and drs.) (4)	Ratio of net benefits to direct costs (Egalitarian preferences) [e] (5)	(Preferences used previously in model) [f] (6)
Nigeria						
Primary school	611	4.76	4,927	987	81.8	16.9
Secondary school	2,910	1.00	1,256	1,256	3.9	3.9
Technical training school	2,713	1.07	1,005	891	2.4	2.1
Form VI	7,356	0.40	−275	−213	0.1	0.3
University	9,130	0.32	2,765	10,537	4.1	8.5
Greece						
Primary	86,959	1.32	25,069	17,438	4.9	3.7
Gymnasium	115,083	1.00	76,139	76,139	14.5	14.5
Lower technical	164,043	0.70	3,830	20,905	1.1	1.6
Lyceum	189,784	0.61	868	5,019	1.2	1.9
University [g]	229,856	0.50	78,245	178,599	4.5	9.1

[a] Column (1) is from column (3) of Table 6 and column (3) of Table 18.
[b] Column (2) is the derivative of the function $E = \log Y$, evaluated at each value of Y, as indicated in column (1); the marginal social utility of income is expressed as a fraction of the value for admittees to secondary school.
[c] Column (3) is the social utility of the net increment in the earnings-stream (column (2) multiplied by the increment in the present value of lifetime earnings, from Tables 6 and 18) minus the direct costs of schooling.
[d] Column (4) is from column (6) of Table 6 and column (6) of Table 18.
[e] Column (5) is column (3) divided by the present value of the direct costs.
[f] Column (6) is from column (7) of Table 6 and column (7) of Table 18.
[g] Refers to humanities and social studies only.

not compelling in any branch of economics. The need for an integrated efficiency and equity model is particularly great in the analysis of education, whose intrinsic functions include both the generation *and* the distribution of income.

Appendixes
Index

Appendix 1 · Data and Sources for Chapter III

1. The Definition of Labor Categories

Labor was grouped in the following categories: those with less than eight years of schooling; those with eight or more, but less than twelve; and those with twelve or more years of schooling. This division corresponds roughly to the usual categories: primary school attendance or less (sometimes, but not in all cases, including those who completed primary school), secondary school attendance (but not completion), and secondary school graduation and above.

Throughout, whenever possible, the earnings of males in their early thirties, rather than the earnings of those of all ages, were used in order to exclude the effects of longer experience and in order to concentrate on earnings differentials associated with additional years spent in schools in the recent past. Since school systems have changed greatly over the last fifty years, the earnings of older workers may reflect exaggerated differences in quality between a year's schooling in one country and the same in another.

A detailed description of the methods used to deal with each country's data can be found in section 3 of the appendix to Samuel Bowles, *The Long-Run Demand for Educated Labor*, Project for Quantitative Research in Economic Development, Harvard University, Economic Development Report No. 89, February 1968. The basic data appear in Table 30.

2. Sources

Belgium

E. F. Denison, *Why Growth Rates Differ: Postwar Experience in Nine Western Countries* (Washington: The Brookings Institute, 1967), pp. 378, 387.

Canada

G. W. Bertram, *The Contribution of Education to Economic Growth*, Economic Council of Canada, Staff Study 12 (Ottawa: Queen's Printer, 1966), p. 48.

J. R. Podoluk, *Earnings and Education* (advance release from the Census Monograph "Incomes of Canadians") (Ottawa: Queen's Printer, 1965), p. 43.

Chile

Marcelo Selowsky, "Education and Economic Growth: Some International Comparisons," unpub. diss., University of Chicago, 1967.

Henry J. Bruton, "The Productivity of Education in Chile" (mimeographed), Research Memo 12, Center for Development Economics, Williams College, Williamstown, Massachusetts, 1967.

Colombia

Marcelo Selowsky, "The Effect of Unemployment and Growth on the Rate of Return to Education: The Case of Colombia," Project for Quantitative Research in Economic Development, Harvard University, Economic Development Report No. 116, 1968.

T. Paul Schultz, *Rate of Return to Education in Bogota, Colombia* (preliminary draft), RAND, January, 1967.

Censo Nacional de Poblacion, 1964.

France

E. F. Denison, *Why Growth Rates Differ*, pp. 376, 385.

Great Britain

Survey of Male Heads of Households by M. Abrams, reported by D. Henderson Stuart in his appendix to Mark Blaug, "Rate of Return on Investment in Education in Great

Britain," *The Manchester School*, September 1965, pp. 253–255.

Census of England and Wales, 1961, Education Tables (London: Her Majesty's Stationery Office, General Register Office, 1966), table 1, p. 1.

Greece

Samuel Bowles, "Sources of Growth in the Greek Economy, 1951–61," and "Changes in the Structure of Employment in Greece by Age, Sex, and Education, 1951–1961," Project for Quantitative Research in Economic Development, Harvard University, Economic Development Report Nos. 27 and 66, 1967.

India

A. M. Nalla Gounden, "Education and Economic Development," unpub. diss., Kurukshetra University, 1965, p. 69.

Marcelo Selowsky, "Education and Economic Growth: Some International Comparisons," Project for Quantitative Research in Economic Development, Harvard University, Economic Development Report No. 83, December 1967.

Census of India, 1961, part II-B (i), General Economic Tables, Table B-I.

Israel

Ruth Klinov-Malul, *The Profitability of Investment in Education in Israel* (Jerusalem: The Maurice Falk Institute for Economic Research in Israel, April, 1966).

Statistical Abstract of Israel, 1957/58, No. 9, Labour and Labour Force, tables 1 and 2.

Mexico

Marcelo Selowsky, "Education and Economic Growth."

Netherlands

E. F. Denison, *Why Growth Rates Differ*, pp. 377–393.

United States

U.S. Census of Population, 1960: PC(2)7B, Subject Reports, Occupation by Earnings and Education, table 1, p. 2.

Dale W. Jorgenson and Zvi Griliches, *The Explanation of*

Productivity Change, Report 6715, Center for Mathematical Studies in Business and Economics, Department of Economics, Graduate School of Business (Chicago: University of Chicago Press, 1967).

Economic Report of the President, 1968 (Washington: U.S. Government Printing Office, 1968).

Table 30. Labor supplies and labor remuneration, selected countries

Country	Year	w_1/w_3	w_2/w_3	Percent of active male labor force			Total males active L [a] (thousands)	National income (millions of 1957 \$) [b]	1958 per capita national income (1957 \$) [c]
				L_1	L_2	L_3			
United States	1959	0.5231	0.7267	15.9	36.3	47.8	46,382	383,858	2,159
Belgium	1961	0.2926	0.4534	18.4	65.3	16.3	2,419	8,458	919
Canada	1960–61	0.4918	0.6522	28.3	47.3	24.4	4,782	24,120	1,323
Chile	1960	0.2521	0.3997	78.6	14.5	6.9	1,854	2,572	335
United Kingdom	1961	0.4868	0.5544	6.6	83.2	10.2	16,254	58,522	1,106
France	1954	0.4034	0.5880	21.9	64.1	14.0	12,097	45,971	996
Greece	1961	0.7038	0.9312	37.0	51.1	11.9	2,458	2,292	273
India	1960–61	0.2961	0.5725	90.0	7.3	2.7	129,042	27,059	64
Mexico	1960	0.1945	0.4460	90.2	7.1	2.7	8,956	9,984	283
Netherlands	1960	0.4499	0.6114	12.8	76.4	10.8	3,231	10,257	881
Colombia	1961	0.2726	0.4855	92.2	41.0	3.8	4,102	2,781	192
Israel	1957	0.3962	0.6607	20.3	44.0	35.7	481	1,565	671

[a] See OECD, *Manpower Statistics, 1950–1962* (Paris: OECD, 1963). For Chile and Mexico, see Marcelo Selowsky, "Education and Economic Growth: Some International Comparisons," Harvard University, Economic Development Report No. 83, 1967.

[b] See *United Nations Yearbook of National Accounts Statistics, 1963* (New York: United Nations, 1964), for figures on national income at constant 1958 prices and for the parity rates employed in converting the figures into 1958 dollars. See U.S. Council of Economic Advisors, *Economic Report of the President, 1968* (Washington: Government Printing Office, 1968), for price index employed in converting the national income figures into dollars of 1957 purchasing power.

[c] For total population figures, see P. N. Rosenstein-Rodan, "International Aid for Underdeveloped Countries," *The Review of Economics and Statistics*, vol. 43, no. 2 (May 1961), pp. 107–138.

Appendix 2 · A Simple Demonstration Model Illustrating the Application of Linear Programming to Educational Planning Problems

Consider a planning problem confined to a single year and to two types of schooling, for example, general secondary education and secondary vocational education. The problem facing the planners is to decide how many students to admit to each of the two types of schools. It will be seen that (given the assumptions of the problem) this is equivalent to determining the distribution of resources between the two types of education. Data on factor supplies and educational technologies are sufficient to determine the set of *feasible* solutions to this problem. The *optimal* solution will depend on our relative valuation of the different outputs of the two schools.

We assume that both schools use the same types of teachers and other professional staff, though in different proportions, and that both use as their intake graduates from primary school. Let there be only two types of teachers, say, science and math teachers and humanities teachers, both of which are in fixed total supply. The total number of available primary school graduates is also given. For simplicity, assume that there are no other inputs. If the required ratio of teachers of each type to the number of students admitted is known—one humanity teacher per fifty admittees in the vocational school, for example—the above information defines a set of feasible educational plans. A *feasible plan* is any combination of admissions to the two schools which does not require more than the available supply of teachers and available primary school graduates.

Let us define X_g and X_v as the number of students admitted to general and vocational schools, respectively. Each type of schooling is referred to as an *activity*, and the magnitude of the admissions is the *activity level*. Further, we define the input coefficients, a_{sg}, a_{sv}, as the number of science and math teachers required per year per hundred admittees to general and to vocational schools, respectively. These input coefficients represent the teacher-student ratio (times 100) for each type of teacher in each school.

The input coefficients a_{hg} and a_{hv} are defined analogously, namely, as the required number of humanities teachers per year per hundred admittees to general and to vocational schools, respectively.

The set of input coefficients for each activity is known as the *technology* of that particular type of school, or its *production function*. Notice that the input coefficients are assumed to be fixed, reflecting the assumed absence of substitution possibilities among school inputs in the production of each type of education. This assumption makes the total number of a given type of teacher required to teach in each school dependent only on the number of students enrolled. For example, the number of humanities teachers required in general secondary schools is $X_g a_{hg}$.

The total number of available science teachers and humanities teachers are T_s and T_h, respectively (the subscripts have the same meaning as above). The total number of primary school graduates available for admission to either school is P.

The problem facing the planners can now be rephrased. The requirement that admissions to general and to vocational schools combined not exceed the available number of primary school graduates can be written:

$$(1) \qquad X_g + X_v \leqq P$$

Likewise, the statement that the admissions to the schools cannot require more than the available number of science and math teachers is:

(2) $\qquad X_g a_{sg} + X_v a_{sv} \leqq T_s$

and, analogously, for humanities teachers:

(3) $\qquad X_g a_{hg} + X_v a_{hv} \leqq T_h$

For obvious reasons, we also require that X_g and X_v must not be negative. This system of three constraint equations has been graphed in Figure 27.

It can be seen at once that an infinite number of combinations of admissions plans is feasible—for example, those represented by points b, c, and d. Thus, the set of feasible plans, known here as the *educational production possibility set*, provides only part of the apparatus necessary for a solution to the problem. In order to choose among the many feasible plans, we need a criterion or *objective function* with which to judge the desirability of each. Let us say that in the view of the planners a year of vocational schooling is twice as socially valuable as a year of general secondary education. Thus, (ignoring dropouts) the planners apparently want to maximize Z, where

(4) $\qquad Z = X_g + 2X_v$

The objective function (4) summarizes the planners' relative valuation of each type of schooling. It is assumed that the relative valuation of the two types of schooling is constant and that it does not depend on the amounts of each type of student produced.

Each plan produces a distinct value of Z; the *optimal plan* is that which produces the highest Z. In this case, by graphing the objective function against the feasible set, we can see that the highest feasible Z is achieved by admitting X_g^* and X_v^*. It is also apparent from the graph that if we had more science and math teachers, represented by an outward shift of equation (2), we could produce a larger value of Z, in this case by admitting more students to vocational schools and fewer students to general schools. (Notice that the possibility of changing the activity levels allows the system to productively use additional mathe-

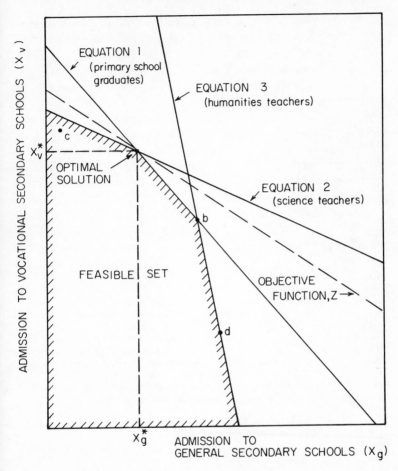

Fig. 27. Geometrical Illustration of a Simple Linear Programming
Model for Education

matics teachers, despite the fact that the individual educational
technologies require that inputs be used in fixed proportions.)
Additional primary school graduates would also allow a higher
Z. But the availability of additional humanities teachers would

produce no change in the solution, as the optimal plan is represented by a point inside the relevant constraint, equation (3): even the initial supply of this type of teacher is not fully employed in the optimal solution.

The increase in the value of Z, the objective function, which is allowed by having one additional unit of a factor of production is the factor's *shadow price*, a concept analogous to the marginal product in general economic analysis.

Linear programming is the name given to a method of formulating and finding the optimum set of activity levels in problems of this sort. The technique also allows the estimation of the shadow price of each input.[1]

This example is overly simple; in actual problems there may be as many as ten distinct types of schooling, and the planning period may extend over a dozen years or more.[2] Many of the simplified aspects of this example, such as the fixed supply of inputs, can be modified.

[1] For additional reading stressing the economic content of linear programming, see: William J. Baumol, *Economic Theory and Operations Analysis,* 2nd ed. (Englewood Cliffs, New Jersey: Prentice-Hall, 1965); Robert Dorfman, Paul A. Samuelson, and Robert M. Solow, *Linear Programming and Economic Analysis* (New York, Toronto, and London: McGraw-Hill Book Co., Inc., 1958). The mathematical structure of the technique is clearly discussed in David Gale, *The Theory of Linear Economic Models* (New York, Toronto, and London: McGraw-Hill Book Co., Inc., 1960); and Clopper Almon, *Matrix Methods in Economics* (Reading, Massachusetts: Addison-Wesley, 1967).

[2] The model prescribed in Chapter V is composed of roughly two hundred activities and four hundred fifty constraints.

Appendix 3 . The Intertemporal Optimizing Model for Education: Basic Equations and Glossary of Notation

1. Objective function:

$$\text{Max } Z = \sum_{j=1}^{m} \sum_{p=1}^{n} X_j^p (Y_j^p - Y_{j'}^p - C_j^p) - \sum_{k=1}^{h} \sum_{p=1}^{n} V_k^p X_k^p$$

   = Present value of contribution of education to future national income

2. Constraints, teachers (one constraint for each year for each type of teacher):

   Teachers of type i required to accommodate the pattern of enrollments in year t *are less than or equal to* teachers surviving from the initial stock *plus* teachers trained within the planning period *plus* former teachers or foreign teachers recruited.

$$\sum_{j=1}^{m} \sum_{p=t+1-s_j}^{t} a_{ij}^t X_j^p \leqq B_i^1 (1 - d_i)^{t-1} + \sum_{p=1}^{t-s_j} g_i X_i^p + X_{i\ast}^t$$

3. Constraints, students (one equation for each type of continuing student in each year):

   Admission to level j in year t *is less than or equal to* output of feeder schools (i) in previous year.

$$\sum_{j=1}^{m} a_{ij}^{t} X_{j}^{t} \leqq g_{i} X_{i}^{t-s_{i}}$$

$$a_{ij}^{t} = \begin{cases} 1 \text{ if } i \text{ is the feeder school for } j \\ 0 \text{ otherwise} \end{cases}$$

4. Constraints, buildings (one equation for each type of building in each year):

   Buildings of type k required by the pattern of enrollments in year t *are less than or equal to* initial stock *plus* new construction since beginning of planning period t.

$$\sum_{j=1}^{m} \sum_{p=t+1-s_{j}}^{t} X_{j}^{p} r_{jk} \leqq B_{k}^{t} + \sum_{p=1}^{t} X_{k}^{p}$$

$$r_{jk} = \begin{cases} 1 \text{ if education } j \text{ uses building of type } k \\ 0 \text{ otherwise} \end{cases}$$

5. Constraints, exogenously supplied resources (one equation for each resource in each year):

   Total use *is less than or equal to* available supply.

$$\sum_{p=t+1-s_{j}}^{t} \sum_{j=1}^{n} X_{j}^{p} a_{ij}^{t} \leqq B_{i}^{t}$$

6. Additional restrictions:

   a) limits on the maximum feasible recruitment or importation of new teachers;
   b) political and administrative feasibility limits—minimum and maximum rates of growth of admission at various levels of schooling.

Appendixes

Notation Glossary

Notation relating to the instrument variables:

X^p_j = the level of activity j in the period p (in most cases the activity level is defined in terms of the number of students admitted).

m = the number of activities.

n = the number of years in the planning period.

h = the number of different types of school buildings.

X^t_{i*} = the amount of resource of type i recruited or imported in period t.

X^p_k = the number of new student places of type k constructed in period p.

Notation relating primarily to the constraint equations:

a^t_{ij} = the minimum input of resource i in period t required to accommodate one student in activity j; $t = 1 \ldots n$, $j = 1 \ldots m$, $i = 1 \ldots m + q$.

q = the number of exogenously supplied inputs.

B^t_i = the amount of resource i available to the system in time t.

s_j = the length of course j in years (similarly defined for s_i).

d_i = the expected annual rate of retirement from the teaching force for teachers of type i.

X^t_{ij} = the amount of input i devoted to activity j in period t.

R^p_{i*} = the upper limit on the recruitment or importation of teachers with qualification i in period p.

Notation relating primarily to the objective function:

Z^p_j = the net benefits function coefficient associated with activity X^p_j .

z   = the row vector ($1 \times nm$) of net benefits coefficients Z_j^p.

Y_j^p = the present value (discounted to year 1) of the stream of income associated with the admission of one student activity j in period p.

$Y_{j'}^p$ = the present value (discounted to year 1) of the alternative earnings-stream, namely, that which would have accrued to the individual had he not received education at activity j.

C_j^p = the present value of the unit recurrent cost of operating activity j in period p.

g_j = the fraction of total admissions to activity X_j expected to complete the course successfully.

Appendix 4 · The Pool of Ability Problem and the Linearity of the Objective Function

It is sometimes feared by educators and others that the average learning aptitude of the student body is inversely related to the magnitude of the student intake. In this case we would expect a fall in the present value of net benefits of each type of schooling as a larger portion of the total population is admitted to each successive level of education. This is the "pool of ability" problem, and it constitutes a possible source of nonlinearity in the objective function.

What is relevant, of course, is not whether the average scholastic (or even expected economic) performance of the student body can be expected to fall with the expansion of admissions. In order for the "pool of ability" to be a problem, it must be shown that the expected *increases* in lifetime productivity due to schooling are larger for the students fortunate enough to be admitted when enrollment is low than for the students who gain admission when enrollment is large. I know of no evidence that this is the case.

Of course, if selection methods were completely rational from an economic standpoint, each child's probability of being admitted would depend directly on the expected gain in his future productivity, and the expected per student economic gain from schooling would depend directly on how many were admitted. But most school systems, thankfully, do not operate this way, but instead pursue admissions policies that seem somewhat more random.[1] In the extreme case of a completely random selection process, no pool of ability problem arises.

The present Northern Nigerian selection methods at both the postprimary and postsecondary levels are probably in large measure unrelated to variables associated with future economic productivity.[2] In view of the apparent low correlation of results on entrance examinations with actual performance in school, there is good reason to assume that the correlation between selection and future economic productivity may be at least equally weak.

Moreover, although we have no information on this point for Greece, evidence from other countries suggests that even where selection criteria more highly correlated with future performance are used and even where a far larger percentage of each age cohort is educated, the pool of ability problem is not likely to be significant.[3]

[1] Of course, self-selection by students and their families for continuation or termination of schooling undoubtedly is based to some extent on the expected future economic gains from schooling.

[2] This view is based on informal personal investigation and on the work of the Nigerian Aptitude Testing Unit in evaluating the validity of the selection methods.

Numerous Nigerian and foreign educators have commented on the arbitrariness of present selection processes. See Paul W. Eberman and Howard E. Wakefield, "An Evaluation of Teacher Education in Northern Nigeria, 1962" (mimeographed) (AID, 1963), p. 29; University of Wisconsin, "The Expansion of Teacher Education in Northern Nigeria, 1961–1970" (mimeographed), report of a study performed by the University of Wisconsin under contract to the Agency for International Development, 1963, p. 35; Michael Goldway, *Report on the Investigation of Vocational Education in Eastern Nigeria* (Jerusalem: State of Israel, 1961), p. 20; K. O. Dike, *et al.*, *Report of the Committee for the Review of the Educational System of Eastern Nigeria* (Enugu: Ministry of Education, 1962), pp. 50–51; UNESCO, "Report of the UNESCO Educational Programming Mission to Nigeria" (mimeographed) (Paris, 1963), p. 68.

[3] Most authors who have treated this problem have dealt with the probable effect of increased admissions on the average quality of the student body rather than with its effect on the average amount learned in school or its effect on the expected increase in productivity due to schooling. Nonetheless, some of the findings are worth citing.

Ingvar Svennilson, "Targets for Education in Europe in 1970," *Policy Conference on Economic Growth and Investment in Education*, vol. II

For the above reasons the pool of ability problem has not been incorporated explicitly into the model. The sensitivity analysis indicates that the results are insensitive to plausible adjustments of the objective function to take account of this phenomenon.

(Paris: OECD, 1962), pp. 34, 38, suggests that in Europe a more rational selection technique can prevent a decline in the quality of student intake or a fall in the expected marginal productivity of the output. Peter DeWolff and K. Harnquist, "Reserves of Ability: Size and Distribution," in A. H. Halsey, *Ability and Educational Opportunity* (Paris: OECD, 1961), p. 141, conclude that even in Sweden, the Netherlands, the U.S., and the U.K., the pool of ability problem is not likely to be serious. Dael Wolfle, in *America's Resources of Specialized Talent: A Current Appraisal and a Look Ahead,* a report to the Commission on Human Resources and Advanced Training (New York: Harper Brothers, 1954), pp. 312–314, indicates that U.S. university enrollments could be significantly increased without a fall in the average I.Q. or high school record of the student intake.

Appendix 5 · Methods of Calculating Incremental Earnings and Costs of Schooling: Greece

PRESENT VALUE OF NET BENEFITS

General Education

Leibenstein's data [1] on earnings in Greece were disaggregated by sex, age, and years of schooling, and average earnings were computed for each cell. Disaggregation by age was based on five-year age categories, while, by years of schooling, it represented those with no schooling at all, successful graduates, and dropouts from each activity. Since educational activities were not differentiable except by the purely numerical years of schooling, university graduates could not be distinguished by their major fields.

The future expected incomes of graduates or dropouts were discounted, multiplied by the appropriate employment rate,[2] and summed over their expected working lifetimes. The resulting figures were then aggregated by the sex ratios [3] and the completion rates [4] associated with the respective educational activities. Here the data allowed a distinction to be made between

[1] Harvey Leibenstein, "Rates of Return to Education in Greece," Development Advisory Service, Harvard University, Economic Development Report No. 94, September 1967.

[2] See Table 31 on Greek employment rates.

[3] National Statistical Service of Greece, *Statistical Yearbook of Greece, 1965* (Athens: Government of Greece, 1966), pp. 102, 116, 123–125.

[4] See Table 32 on wastage and retardation.

Table 31. Employment rates, Greece, 1961

Level of schooling	Age (years)						
	10–14	15–19	20–24	25–29	30–44	45–64	65+
Male							
Not finished primary and illiterate	0.740	0.878	0.560	0.926	0.938	0.866	0.434
Primary	0.737	0.874	0.558	0.922	0.934	0.862	0.432
Secondary	—	0.798	0.509	0.841	0.852	0.786	0.394
Higher	—	—	0.541	0.895	0.907	0.837	0.420
Female							
Not finished primary and illiterate	0.430	0.575	0.548	0.443	0.396	0.322	0.101
Primary	0.330	0.440	0.420	0.339	0.303	0.247	0.077
Secondary	—	0.420	0.400	0.323	0.288	0.235	0.074
Higher	—	—	0.900	0.727	0.649	0.529	0.166

Source: Samuel Bowles, "Changes in the Structure of Employment in Greece by Age, Sex, and Education, 1951–1961," Project for Quantitative Research in Economic Development, Harvard University, Economic Development Report No. 66, February 1967.

university graduates oriented toward the humanities and social sciences and those oriented toward mathematics and the natural sciences. These aggregated figures are entered in Table 18 as "present value of lifetime earnings."

Technical Education

Lower Technical Schools. From the original Leibenstein data, observations on males with a primary school education or its equivalent were isolated. Regressions on this set of data yielded:

$$(1) \quad Y = 180.98A - 1.93A^2 + 198.84T + 459.45Q - 1775.44$$
$$\quad (15.54) \quad (-12.54) \quad (6.80) \quad (8.33) \quad (-8.46)$$
$$R^2 = .38 \qquad \text{degrees of freedom} = 835$$

where the figures in parentheses are t-values, and Y denotes monthly income; A, age; T, years of technical education; and Q, year index of observation. Annual income is considered equiva-

Table 32. Wastage and retardation rates in Greece, 1961–1962

Type of schooling	Fraction of students entering expected to complete course	Length of studies	
		Average	Nominal
Primary			
Male	0.99	6.6	6
Female	0.98	6.6	6
Gymnasium			
Male	0.62	3.5	3
Female	0.83	3.5	3
Lyceum			
Male	0.79	3.6	3
Female	0.91	3.5	3
Lower Technical			
Male	0.77	3.1	3
Female	0.63	3.2	3
Secondary Technical			
Male	0.86	3.3	3
Female	0.81	3.2	3
Higher			
Arts, humanities			
Male	0.91	4.8	4
Female	0.68	4.8	4
Physics, mathematics			
Male	0.38	4.9	4
Female	0.40	4.9	4
Engineering			
Male	0.94	4.4	4
Female	0.89	4.4	4
Pedagogical Academies			
Male	0.96	3.1	3
Female	0.98	3.1	3

Source: Samuel Bowles, "Wastage and Retardation in Greek Education—Preliminary Estimates," unpub., September 1966.

lent to 11.5 times monthly income. Setting $T = 0$, we obtain the expected earnings of a successful male graduate of primary education; $T = 3$ implies a successful male graduate of a lower technical school. To make these results comparable to those in the first part of Appendix 5, the discounted sums obtained from this equation were multiplied by the ratio of the discounted sum calculated previously for a successful male primary school graduate to the discounted sum obtained from the equation with $T = 0$.

Polytechnical University. From the original Leibenstein data, observations on males whose total years of schooling were the equivalent of a university education were isolated. Regression on this sample data yielded:

$$(2) \quad Y = 400.40A - 3.15A^2 + 1647.47\emptyset + 1421.01Q - 6282.34$$
$$\quad\quad (2.96) \ (-2.00) \quad\quad (3.65) \quad\quad (3.74) \quad\quad (-2.29)$$
$$\quad\quad R^2 = .23 \quad\quad\quad\quad\quad\quad\quad \text{degrees of freedom} = 271$$

where, as before, Y, A, and Q denote monthly income, age, and the year index, respectively; $\emptyset$ is an occupation index, differentiating technical and nontechnical occupations. ($\emptyset$ takes the value 1 or 0, depending on whether the observation holds a technical or a nontechnical job.) I assumed that all polytechnical school graduates subsequently enter technical occupations. The discounted sum of the annual equivalents obtained from the above equation is entered in Table 18 as "Present value of lifetime earnings." To the extent that not all graduates of polytechnical institutions obtain technical jobs, the earnings-stream for engineering and related fields is probably an overestimate.

PRESENT VALUE OF LIFETIME EARNINGS FOREGONE

To compute the foregone earnings associated with each educational activity, using the sex weights of that activity, the discounted sums of those who had successfully completed the immediately preceding activity were aggregated. Thus, for example, the foregone earnings of a primary school graduate are the sum of total earnings of those with no education weighted by the sex ratios of primary education.

Present Value of Direct Recurrent Social Costs

The derivation of these figures is described in the text. Entry in this column of Table 18 for lower technical, however, includes the three-year sum of annual rental charges for technical school buildings. (This procedure was adopted because of the high percentage of all technical school facilities that are rented.) The annual charge is the estimated cost per student place times the sum of the discount rate and a 3 percent depreciation rate; this charge is in turn discounted and summed over the relevant three-year period. Thus, to accommodate one student through a lower technical school, it is not necessary to build one student place; no entries are made in a building constraint; instead, annual charges are accrued and entered only in the expenditure constraint.

Marginal Costs of Recruiting Activities

Earnings of teachers when the maximum number are recruited (w_M)

Primary school teachers. From the disaggregation used in the first section of Appendix 5, the earnings of male and female observations, aged 30–34, and with years of schooling equivalent to that of a pedagogical academy graduate were weighted and summed according to the sex composition of the primary school teaching staff.[5]

Secondary school teachers in the nonscientific subjects. From the same disaggregation, male and female observations, age category 30–34, and years of schooling equivalent to that of a uni-

[5] *Statistical Yearbook of Greece, 1965,* pp. 102, 104.

versity were weighted and summed with weights computed from the sex composition of secondary nonscience teaching staff.

Secondary school teachers in the sciences. The costs for this group were approximated by the same method as for secondary school teachers in nonscientific subjects, using earnings data for males only.

University professors in the humanities and the social sciences. In equation (2), above, the maximum Y, for those in nontechnical occupations, with ($\varnothing = 0$), represents the highest earnings category for a nonscience university graduate and the approximate cost for recruiting qualified personnel as university professors.

University professors in the sciences and engineering. From the same equation, the maximum earnings, with $\varnothing = 1$, was used.

Present Salaries (w_P)

Average salaries of teachers in the primary and secondary schools were computed from the total public expenditures on primary and secondary education and the total number of teachers in each.[6] For university professors, because of a lack of information on the full-time equivalents of university teaching staff, the monthly incomes obtained from equation (2) were multiplied by 10.0 instead of 11.5 as rough estimates of their annual earnings from work done within the university alone.

Marginal Costs of Recruitment (MC)

As described in the text, the maximum allowable levels of recruitment for the first year were equal to the number of teachers in the schools in 1961. Thus, the maximum possible availability assumed in this calculation, b_M, is twice the initial availability, b_P, Assuming a constant marginal cost for each recruitment activity, the following relationship is readily obtained:

[6] Mediterranean Regional Project, *Country Reports, Greece* (Paris: OECD, 1965), pp. 77, 94.

$$MC = \frac{b_M w_M - b_P w_P}{b_M - b_P}$$

where b_P and b_M denote the present constraint level and the projected maximum total availability, that is, maximum recruitment plus initial stock; w_P and w_M, respectively, denote the average wage and the wages of teachers when the maximum number is recruited.

Substituting $b_M = 2b_P$,

$$MC = 2w_M - w_P.$$

The marginal costs for years 2 . . . 14 of the planning period were adjusted upward by the 3 percent per annum expected rate of productivity growth, and discounted at 10 percent. See Table 33.

Table 33. Marginal costs of recruiting teachers in Greece, 1961

Teachers	Cost (drachmas)
Primary school	38,104
Secondary school	
Humanities and social sciences	30,127
Natural sciences	40,043
University	
Humanities and social sciences	173,859
Mathematics and physical sciences	195,276
Polytechnical university	195,276

THE AVAILABLE STOCK OF TEACHERS AND POTENTIAL RECRUITS

The available stock of teachers of each type in each year is the stock existing in 1961 minus expected retirements, plus all graduates of the pedagogical academy (primary school teachers) and a fraction of the graduates of the various university faculties. In addition to the available stock, which may be hired at the existing and projected salary schedules, there is a pool of poten-

Table 34. Maximum fraction of university graduates assumed available
as teachers: Greece

Branch of education	Available at planned salary levels		Potential recruits at higher salary levels	
	High school	University [a]	High school	University
Physical sciences and mathematics	0.10	0.01	0.10	0.05
Humanities and social sciences	0.20	0.01	0.20	0.05
Engineering and related subjects	—	0.01	—	0.05

[a] The university graduates who may become university teachers are available only after seven years from the time of their admission to the university.

tial recruits who may be induced to teach by a higher salary schedule. This pool was assumed to be as large as the number of teachers employed in 1961 plus a fraction of the outputs of the university. The fraction of university graduates who enter the available stock of teachers or the pool of potential recruits is indicated in Table 34.

Index

Index

Terminal conditions of educational growth, 109, 167-172

Tinbergen, Jan: model of educational planning, 144-152; assumptions, 179-181; costs, 188-189; goals, 189-191

Unemployment rates, 16, 48

United States: growth of general education, 4-5; expenditures, 6; age-earnings profiles, 12

Wastage. *See* Drop-outs and

Wealth of Nations, 1-2

Weisbrod, Burton, 166

Welch, Finis, 56

Williams, Gareth: study of Greek education, 145-152

H-K18